Retro Fiesta

A Gringo's Guide to Mexican Party Planning

Geraldine Duncann

Portland, Oregon

Designer: Mary Ruhl

Editors: Sue Mann & Lisa Perry

Library of Congress Cataloging-in-Publication Data

Duncann, Geraldine.

Retro Fiesta : A Gringo's Guide to Mexican Party Planning / by Geraldine Duncann.-- 1st American ed.

p. cm.

Includes index.

ISBN 1-933112-01-8 (hardcover : alk. paper)

1. Cookery, Mexican. 2. Parties. I. Title.

TX716.M4D88 2005

642'.4--dc22

2005002119

Printed in Singapore

9 8 7 6 5 4 3 2 1

Collectors Press books are available at special discounts for bulk purchases, premiums, and promotions. Special editions, including personalized inserts or covers, and corporate logos, can be printed in quantity for special purposes. For further information contact: Special Sales, Collectors Press, Inc., P.O. Box 230986, Portland, OR 97281. Toll free: 1-800-423-1848.

For a free catalog write:

Collectors Press, Inc.

P.O. Box 230986

Portland, OR 97281

Toll free: 1-800-423-1848

collectorspress.com

Retro Fiesta is part of the Retro series by Collectors Press.

Dedication

To the memory of our little Mhari this book is dedicated.

Contents

Introduction

When I was a kid we lived in Lake Elsinore in southern California — no Danish castle, just Aimee Semple McPherson's summer retreat. Baja California and the exotic delights of Tijuana were an easy day trip for us and we went there often . . . well, as often as our gas-ration stamps would allow. My dad did the milking a little early those mornings, and the poor cow waited a little later those nights.

In the 1940s Tijuana seemed the most exotic, colorful, and romantic place on earth. Narrow side streets hosted a jumble of tiny shops and street stalls. Pottery stood in teetering stacks by the shop where my mother bought a colorful set of dinnerware made in Oaxaca. Because I was growing so fast, I got a new pair of huaraches almost every time we went. I loved the heavy scent of new leather in the shop selling shoes, belts, and purses.

And speaking of smells . . . the smell of roasting meats, of onions, garlic, cumin, chocolate, and coffee was everywhere. When we passed the open door of the cantina, cool air heavy with the scent of stale beer and tobacco drifted out. Once when I peeked in, I saw big two-bladed fans gently swishing round and round in the gloomy interior, just like in Casablanca.

For some reason we were never afraid of getting the turistas, the Aztec Two-Step, or Montezuma's Revenge, those devastating disorders that plague most visitors. We ate everything. A plethora of exotic foods beckoned to us from street venders' stalls and carts: tiny soft tacos stuffed with grilled meats and dripping with onions and salsa, skewers of meats sizzling on makeshift grills, little taquitos, and warm soft tamales. One vender sold huge cucumbers sliced lengthwise and sprinkled with vinegar, salt, and cayenne pepper, then wrapped in wax paper and handed to you. Another sold exotic candies. No Snickers or Three Musketeers here — just candied yams, cactus candy, candied coconut, and pinocci. And oh, the strawberry man! A wizened man always stood on the same corner selling huge, twisted white paper cones filled with the tiniest wild strawberries, none larger than a thumbnail, sprinkled with powdered sugar and cinnamon, if you wanted. This wonderful delight cost twenty-five cents!

Sometimes instead of going to Tijuana we went up to Los Angeles and killed two cultural birds with one stone. We went to the Grand Central Market on Fourth Street in old Los Angeles to buy huge loaves of blacker-than-black Jewish-Russian rye bread and real pastrami, then visited nearby Olvera Street for the rest of the day and into the evening. Colorful Olvera Street was perhaps even more exciting to me than Tijuana because it was the whole shebang condensed into one block.

As an adult I have made numerous trips to the interior of Mexico, which I have always enjoyed immensely — always learning a lot, always finding it exciting and thrilling. But somehow it never quite recaptured the magic of those early days, those first exotic adventures. Perhaps it's because of a child's exaggerated memory, but I think it was because of the era. America was tired of the war, tired of rationing, tired of khaki and olive drab. Mexico offered a welcome relief, an opulence of colors, tastes, and smells. Is it any wonder that postwar America fell in love with her neighbor?

That love affair was aided by the movies: light-hearted films like *Mexican Spitfire* starring Lupe Velez, which showed us the superficial Mexico we wanted to see. Even Andy Hardy took a trip to Mexico, and in glorious black-and-white! Who will forget the line, "Badges, what badges? I don gots to show jew no stinkin' badges" from *The Treasure of the Sierra Madre.* A bit later we lost our hearts to *The Brave One*, this time in full color. Performers like Carmen Miranda and Carlos Montalban kept us enthralled with their south of the border capers. It didn't matter that Carmen was from Brazil and Carlos from Argentina. For whatever reason, postwar America was fascinated with Mexico and things Mexican or almost Mexican, and it is to the celebration of that era this book is dedicated.

That "South of the Border" Feel

Creating Atmosphere, Planning

Getting Started

When: Just about any time — summer, winter, daytime, evening, indoors or out. Some dates, however, are particularly appropriate.

January 1: Año Nuevo (New Year's Day) This is an official Mexican holiday.

January 6: Diá de los Santos Reys (Epiphany, 12 days after Christmas) This is the date when, according to tradition, the three wise men arrived in Bethlehem with their gifts for the Christ Child. In the early days of the Christian calendar, Christmas was a day of religious observance; Epiphany (Twelfth Night) was the day for gift giving, feasting, and celebration.

January 17: Feast Day of de San Antonio de Abad During this religious holiday, the Catholic Church allows animals to be brought to into church to be blessed. It is a colorful celebration; many people clean and brush their animals and dress them with garlands of flowers and the like.

February 5: Dia de la Constitución This official holiday celebrates Mexico's constitution.

February 24: Flag Day This national holiday honors Mexico's flag.

February–March: Carnaval This floating holiday is a celebration of excess before Lent.

March 21: Birthday of Benito Juárez This official holiday celebrates the birth of one of Mexico's most famous presidents and national heroes.

Semana Santa: This holy week that ends Lent includes Good Friday and Easter Sunday. It is a Mexican custom to break cascarones (see page 14) over your friends' heads.

May 1: Primero de Mayo (May Day) May Day is a national holiday in Mexico, equivalent to our Labor Day.

May 5: Cinco de Mayo This celebrates Mexico's victory over the French in 1842, instrumental in leading to Mexico's independence.

May 10: Día de Madres (Mother's Day) Because of the importance of mothers in Mexican culture, this official holiday has special significance.

June 1: Día de Armada (Navy Day) This holiday is a day off in Mexico.

September 8: Dia de Nuestra Señora (Day of Our Lady) This local Baja, California, holiday celebrates its first mission.

September 16: Mexican Independence Day This important holiday celebrates the day Miguel Hidalgo proclaimed the Mexican revolt against Spanish rule.

October 12: Dia de la Raza (Day of the Race) This day celebrates Columbus's arrival in the Americas and the historical origins of the Mexican race.

November 1, 2: Dia de los Muertos (Day of the Dead) This very important holiday combines Europe's All Saints Day and the Aztec worship of the dead to make a two-day celebration of departed loved ones.

November 20: Mexican Revolution Day This official holiday celebrates Mexico's Revolution of 1910.

December 12: Dia de Nuestra Señora de Guadalupe (Day of Our Lady of Guadalupe) This is the feast day of Mexico's patron saint, the Virgin of Guadalupe, and is celebrated with great fervor.

December 16–January 6: Las Posadas (The Processions) This religious holiday commemorates Joseph and Mary's search for shelter in Bethlehem, celebrated with candlelight processions that end at nativity scenes, then at someone's house for feasting and other festivities, sort of like caroling parties.

December 25: Navidad (Christmas Day)

Setting the Scene

Whether you're planning a small dinner party or a backyard bash, most of your success depends on setting the scene, so think color! Mexico vibrates with the hot, wonderful color of desert and tropical flowers, strikingly plumed birds, bougainvillea-covered stucco walls, terra-cotta roofs, azure seas, striped serapes, and garlands of chiles.

Fabric: Swaths of inexpensive fabric in red, white, and green, the colors of the Mexican flag, introduce color to your fiesta. Use them as tablecloths and on windows, swag them on walls; use them outside as canopies, draperies, and pennants.

Crepe paper: Streamers are available in craft stores. Buy them in the colors of the flag, twist them together, and put them up with the aid of a ladder, push pins, and your imagination.

Serapes: The colorful woven blankets of Mexico can add greatly to your atmosphere. Throw them over the sofa or use as wall hangings. Use inexpensive solid-color fabric for the tablecloth and a serape for the table runner. But be careful: Put something under your serving dishes and candlesticks to catch the drips — serapes are neither inexpensive nor washable (they're made of wool).

Flowers: Large, brilliant crepe-paper and tissue-paper flowers are available in Mexican specialty shops. However, when possible use fresh, large bouquets of sunflowers, zinnias, corn flowers, and cosmos as well as potted geraniums and cactus.

Riestras: Hanging riestras, or chile garlands, are another wonderful way to bring the color of Mexico into your home. Making traditional riestras, however, can be tedious and expensive because each one requires several pounds of dried chilies. You can cheat and use a large tapestry needle and heavy twine to make strings of fresh chiles, or look online to find manufactured alternatives.

Lighting: Lighting is a vital part of setting the scene. Use strings of Christmas lights that look like chiles. Make your own candle lanterns. Fill large tin cans with Styrofoam or florists' blocks of foam. If your can has a lid, tape it on securely and fill the can with sand. Use a hammer and nails to pierce a pattern of small holes in the cans. Pierced tinwork is a tradition in Mexico.

HAPPY BIRTHDAY! It's just an old SPANISH CUSTOM...

And gee ---- make no mistake, I hope this finds you HAVING FUN...

Table Settings

Mexican pottery: Using Mexican pottery for serving pieces can bring authenticity to your fiesta table, but be warned: Much of it contains white lead in its glaze, which is poisonous.

To determine if your pottery is unsafe, put a tablespoon or two of distilled vinegar or fresh lemon juice in the bottom of the pottery. Let it sit overnight. In the morning if there is no discoloration, the piece is okay to use. If there is discoloration, the piece has enough white lead in it to be dangerous. Do not store acidic food (tomatoes, lemons, etc.) in these dishes and do not cook in them. Chips and other dry foods can be displayed safely, however.

And don't forget vintage and reproduction Fiesta dishes. Their warm corals, turquoises, and golds add a wonderful touch.

Makeshift serving pieces: When serving a gang, you may not have enough large serving pieces. Baskets, trays, and even pieces of plywood can all become make-do serving pieces. Scrub them; cover with aluminum foil or plastic wrap; cover that with lettuce or cabbage leaves, kale, parsley, banana leaves, or other edible, nontoxic greenery; and pile on your food. Don't forget nontoxic flowers for garnishing plates and platters; roses, marigolds, calendulas, pansies, borage blossoms, and nasturtiums are all appropriate. Organic mint leaves, bay leaves, and other fresh herbs can also work.

Inexpensive disposable aluminum plates and trays provide another option and are available in most groceries. Give them the greenery and flower treatment as well.

Glassware: Beautiful blue bubble glassware made in Mexico is usually available in import stores and in housewares shops. They add sparkle to your fiesta setting. They can be expensive, however, so I would reserve them for smaller events and use disposable plastic for larger bashes.

Linens: Use inexpensive fabric for quick and attractive table napkins. Tear the fabric into appropriate-size squares and hem them, or fringe them and leave them unhemmed. You can find a wide selection of colorful and decorative paper napkins as well.

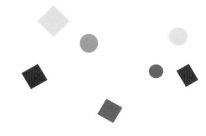

Grande Fun & Games

Some people enjoy arranged activities at parties; others just like to eat, drink, and converse. If your friends do indeed like games and activities, you may enjoy using some of the following suggestions.

Pass the Pepper: You'll need one red bell pepper and one green bell pepper — both large and firm. Stand your guests in two lines. Give the first person in one line a red pepper and the first person in the other line a green pepper. Each person puts the pepper under his or her chin, then tries to pass it to the next person in line. No one may use hands, just chins. The team that gets the pepper to the end of the line is the winner.

Huevos Casca (Cracking the Eggs): Provide brightly colored hard-boiled eggs in a basket. Each guest writes his or her name on one egg and puts it back in the basket. Shake the basket a few seconds and remove eggs that have cracked. Then shake it again and remove the cracked eggs, continuing until only one uncracked egg remains. The guest whose name is on the egg gets a prize.

Cascarones: Cascarones are colored eggshells filled with confetti. Fill several baskets with cascarones and put them here and there. Guests pick up the cascarones and crack them on each others' heads. If the confetti cascades instead of staying in a pile on top of the head, the recipient will have good luck. The one breaking the cascarone must make a wish beforehand, and if the confetti cascades, the wish will come true.

To make cascarones: Dye eggs with food coloring or paint them; allow to dry. Use a needle to make a small hole in one end of the egg; use needle again to create a 1/2-inch hole in the other end. Blow on the small hole to empty the insides. Rinse the empty shells well and allow to dry thoroughly. Use a funnel to fill egg with confetti (tissue paper type is best). Glue a piece of bright colored tissue paper over the larger hole to keep in the confetti.

Piñatas: Piñatas are known around the world as Mexico's gift to party-goers, fiestas, and celebrations. Filled with candies, small toys, and other treats, colorful piñatas have brought joy to children and adults alike for generations. Here's the traditional way to break the piñata: Everyone stands in a line. The first person is blindfolded, spun around three times, then given a stick with which to break the piñata. That person has only three tries; then the next person has three tries. This continues until someone breaks it, at which time there is a scramble to retrieve the goodies that were inside. The one who broke it usually gets a special prize. Piñatas are readily available in many stores; however, it is lots of fun to make your own.

Making a piñata is easy but can be a bit tedious. When making a piñata at home forget about making the animal-shaped ones. You'll likely wind up going nutty. The easiest one to make is a simple globe-shaped piñata using a filled balloon as a base.

To make your piñata, you will need:

several days — the project must dry between stages

a place to hang your creation while you are working

sharp craft scissors

newspaper (not the glossy pages) or paper towels

1 large bottle white glue (like Elmer's)

water

1 large balloon, blown up to desired size

string or twine

brightly colored tissue paper

filling (small toys, wrapped candies, nuts, etc.)

brightly colored yarn or ribbons

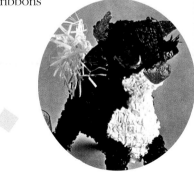

Inflate and tear or cut a bunch of newspapers into 1 x 12-inch strips. Put 1 part glue and 3 parts water in a large flat bowl. Tie string around end of balloon and hang over workspace at a comfortable height. Begin by dipping a strip of paper into the diluted glue. Using your fingers as a squeegee to remove excess glue. Lay strip on the balloon and smooth out well. Continue until the entire surface of the balloon is covered with paper and allow to dry thoroughly (usually overnight). The next day add another layer of paper strips and dry overnight. Continue in this manner until you have at least 4 layers. When piñata is dry, take it down and puncture the balloon. Draw a line around the piñata about 2 to 3 inches down from the hole where the tail of the balloon was. Using scissors or a knife, cut along this line to make an opening for filling the piñata. Add filling and use more strips of paper and glue to cover the opening. Allow to dry. Cut tissue paper into 2 x 12-inch strips. Fold strips over several times and fringe the paper along the long side with scissors. Begin at the bottom of the piñata and glue strips on in concentric circles about an inch apart, working up until the entire piñata is covered. You may find it easier to work if the piñata is hanging. To hang, punch 3 or 4 evenly spaced holes about 2 inches down from the opening and thread bright colored yarn or ribbons through them. When the piñata is completely covered with tissue paper, allow it to dry thoroughly before filling. Be careful not to fill with heavy goodies or the ties may rip through the holes.

A much easier version, which is just as much fun if not as traditional and attractive, is to double or triple brown paper bags. Fill them with goodies, tie them shut, and decorate with glued strips of brightly colored fringed tissue or crepe paper.

The Mime Game: This is an age-old party game somewhat related to charades. When your guests arrive, pin either a picture or a word on their backs. Throughout the party people come up to them and try to mime the picture or word. At some point your guests try to guess what was on their backs based on the miming antics of the other guests. And no fair looking in a mirror!

Salsa: We all love salsa and think ours is the best. Why not have a salsa competition? Guests can make their entries at home and bring them for judging. Afterward, put them on the buffet table for all to enjoy. Better make two categories: mild and son-of-a-gun!

Carmen Miranda: Remember the fantastic headdresses Carmen sported in most of her films? Have a Carmen Miranda competition who can create and wear the most outlandish Carmen Miranda headdress.

Badges: Everyone knows that line from The Treasure of the Sierra Madre. Whoever says "Badges, what badges? I don gots to show jew no stinkin' badges" best gets a prize. Sponsor a contest for the best bandito look-alike or for the character Bogart played in *The Treasure of the Sierra Madre*. Foolish but fun.

The Limbo: Although the limbo originated in the Caribbean and is usually thought of in combination with the calypso era, it is nontheless lots of fun and a great icebreaker, particularly if you can find the original limbo music.

Latin Melody: Salsa dancing may be all the rage now, but this isn't a "now" party. It's a retro party, so drag out some of the oldies. In the postwar era Americans were crazy for such south of the border dances as the samba, the mambo, the tango, the Mexican Hat Dance, and that greatest icebreaker of all, the conga line. Not all are Mexican, but they sure are fun and are about as retro as it gets.

Useful Spanish Words

Adios (ah-dee-ohss): goodbye

Amiga (ah-mee-gah): friend, female

Amigo (ah-mee-goh): friend, male

Baño (bahn-yoh): bathroom

Bienvenidos (bee-en-veh-nee-dohss): welcome

Casa (cah-sah): home

Comida (coh-mee-dah): food

Como estas (coh-moh es-stahss): how are you

Estoy satisfecho (es-stoy sah-tees-fay-choh): I'm full

Fiesta (fee-es-tah): party, holiday

Grande (grahn-day): big

Gracias (grah-see-ahss): thank you

Hola (oh-lah): hello or hi

Hombre (ohm-bray): man

Me llamo (may yah-moh): my name is…

Mesa (may-sah): table

Mujer (moo-hair): woman

Niña (neen-yah): child, female

Niño (neen-yoh): child, male

No (noh): no

Picante (pee-cahn-tay): hot (spicy)

Por favor (poor fah-vor): please

Sabroso (sah-broh-soh): tasty

Si (see): yes

Sombrero (sohm-breh-roh): hat

Cool As a Margarita for Party Time

Shopping So You Won't Go Crazy

First: Peruse your recipes and decide on a menu. Set it aside, think about it for a while, peruse your recipes again, and finalize the menu. This can take several days and may include a trip to the market to see what's available.

Second: After you set the menu, write down the ingredients you need for each recipe.

Third: Check your pantry for staples you'll need, like flour, sugar, baking powder, salt, pepper, and herbs and spices. If I assume I have the ingredients, when I start cooking — oops!

Fourth: Begin compiling your shopping list. Put the ingredients you need to buy in categories: eggs and dairy, meat, produce, staples, and so on. Keep a tally by each ingredient to note each time you will be using it in a recipe. For example, if I'll be using two eggs in four recipes, I make eight marks by "eggs" on my shopping list.

Fifth: Usually I can't get everything I need at one store. So I redo the shopping list to reflect not only categories but also categories by store. This is a very helpful and efficient planning method!

Sixth: I decide which items I can buy earlier in the week — flour, sugar, oil, butter, potatoes, onions — thereby reducing my load when I do the major shopping. That way I need to worry about only the fresh things on the day I do my major shopping, usually as early in the morning as possible on the day before the event.

Seventh: Decide if anything needs to be picked up the day of the event, and determine if someone else can pick it up for you. Ice most definitely falls into this category.

What to Do with it All

Most of today's homes are not set up to accommodate an influx of groceries. Create temporary storage using card tables to set things on and ice chests for produce that won't fit into your refrigerator. Categorizing ingredient storage assists in revealing anything that's missing.

In What Can I Cook All That ?

Start calling friends for their pots and baking dishes, or head for thrift stores. It doesn't matter if a lid doesn't fit or if a pot doesn't even have a lid. Aluminum foil serves as a fine lid, while disposable aluminum foil baking pans can accommodate a number of dishes with the varieties of shapes and sizes carried by most supermarkets.

Cooking Sequentially

Decide which recipes you can make ahead — usually most of the baking, the sauces and salsas, and the marinades for meats. You can marinate most meats the day before the party. Roast peppers, chiles, and garlic in advance; they'll keep in the fridge several days.

Cut-up and blanched vegetables can be done the day before and refrigerated. Some people tear lettuce for salads, put them in plastic bags, and keep them in the fridge or ice chest. However, because preparing lettuce doesn't take very long, I prefer to do it just before serving.

Helping Hands

You will probably need some help preparing your party fare, particularly toward the end when you are in the final push. Most people want to help, but for many this means hanging out in the kitchen to chat. Enlist a trusted friend or two who can be of significant help. Give them badges that identify them as kitchen helpers and post signs on all kitchen doors that politely ask guests to please stay out of there! I know it may seem rather rude, but believe me, without it you may just commit murder.

One of your biggest entertainment aids is someone who acts as host or hostess until you are through with your kitchen duties: husband, wife, adult kid, roommate, or friend. After you have everything on the table, then you can relax, have a drink, and enjoy the day.

Mucho Eats & Cooking Feats

These recipes are not the last word on Mexican cooking. In no way is this blonde, blue-eyed gringo making any claims to be an expert on the cuisines of our south of the border neighbors. The recipes here are adaptations of Mexican-American recipes typical in the Latino communities of the postwar Southwest.

Tex-Mex, you may say. However, as a fifth-generation Californian, I take great exception to the concept that all Mexican-American food is Tex-Mex. My family was cooking Mexican-influenced food, cooked in Mexican pottery made on my great-grandfather's cattle ranch by Mexican workers long before some food writer-journalist ever coined the phrase "Tex-Mex." I think the only reason the term became so popular is that it rhymes.

Lard vs. Olive Oil

Yes, totally authentic Mexican food does indeed use lard as its major fat source; however, in most cases I substituted olive oil when a recipe called for lard. This change, incidentally, is becoming a trend even in Mexico. If you think your arteries won't mind too much, use lard instead of olive oil in any recipe.

Chile Powder and Italian Seasoning

When a recipe calls for chile powder, I am talking about the seasoning blend you put in chile, not plain cayenne. Although chile powder was invented in the United States, it wouldn't have been developed if it weren't for cross-cultural influences. Chile powder is a good basic Mexican-influenced seasoning blend that works well as a shortcut in many dishes.

Servings

The number of servings depends greatly on the people you are serving. A group of slim, dieting ladies will require different quantities than your teenage son's soccer team, but doubling or tripling recipes is easy to do. However, don't automatically double or triple the quantities of seasonings and spices. Always add them by taste because most seasonings, not believing in mathematical laws, often like to play games with you.

Chiles

Most standard markets don't name chiles at all; they're simply in a bin marked Small Hot Chiles, Large Mild Chiles, or just Chiles. When a recipe calls for fresh chiles and you cannot find them, fresh bell peppers and dry chile flakes to taste are adequate substitutes. Tabasco-style hot sauce is not an automatic substitute for chiles. It will add heat, but it is a fermented product that is quite sour as well as hot, and you won't want that quality in many recipes.

In general I call for jalapeños and serranos, both small hot chiles, and Anaheims, which are large, long chiles sometimes called Italian or stuffing chiles.

NOTE: Avoid injury to hands and eyes by utilizing proper chile handling. Many cookbooks suggest wearing gloves while cutting, but I don't trust this method. I'd probably chop off my finger. Don't touch your eyes or other areas until your hands are thoroughly cleaned. After cutting, wash your hands, cutting board, and utensils with soap and water, then wipe them with acidulated water — 1 cup cold water mixed with about 1/4 cup lemon juice or vinegar. Let sit a minute or so, then wipe with clear water to remove the acid.

Ice

For some recipes like chilled soup or punch, you'll need a block of ice. Make your own in large yogurt or cottage cheese containers. There's an added benefit: you can decorate the block by freezing lime, lemon, or orange slices in the center. Just wait until the block is partly frozen to add the fruit. This prevents them from floating to the top.

Comal and Metate

A comal is a flat terra-cotta or metal disk with handle that is placed over a stove burner to warm tortillas and toast dried chiles. A cast-iron skillet will do the same thing. A matate is a grinding stone used for mixing and grinding seasoning blends. Your blender is a reasonable substitute.

These two items are indispensable in Mexican kitchens, but you certainly don't need them to make an excellent Mexican meal.

Apertivus

Appetizers

I Made Them Myself Tortilla Chips

vegetable oil for deep frying

electric deep fryer, large heavy pot,
  or wok to deep fry in

corn or flour tortillas

deep-frying thermometer

wire rack

clean brown paper bags

salt, to taste

Put 3–4 inches oil in deep fryer. If using electric deep fryer, follow manufacturer's directions. Heat oil to deep frying temperature. Cut tortillas into whatever size wedges you wish using large sharp knife. (I usually use 6-inch tortillas and cut them into eighths.) Carefully drop in one or two tortilla wedge, they should sink into oil, rapidly float to surface, and begin to brown. Using slotted spoon or wire scooper, remove chips when they are light golden brown. Put on rack to drain; sprinkle with salt while still hot. Continue until all chips are cooked. Don't put more chips in oil at a time than you can comfortably work with. If you add too many, they will be overcrowded and may stick together,

they can cool the oil, you won't be able to remove them from the oil before some become too brown, and they may cause the oil to boil over. When chips finish draining, put them in brown bags, which will continue to absorb excess oil. Now all you need is good salsa, such as Basic Salsa Fresca Rojo (see page 37), San Joaquin Salsa Crudo (see page 37), or Salsa Verde (see page 41).

Glorious Guacamole

3 to 4 ripe avocados,

1 medium yellow onion, minced

1 green onion including green, chopped finely

2 to 3 cloves garlic, minced

1 tomato, finely diced

1/4 cup fresh cilantro, minced, plus fresh sprig for garnish

1 scant tsp sugar

1 fresh jalapeño chile, seeded and minced, to taste*

fresh lime juice, to taste, plus wedge for garnish

salt and black pepper, to taste

Cut each avocado in half, remove seed, and scoop out all meat. Put meat into bowl and mash well with fork. Add remaining ingredients, mix well, and place in serving bowl. Garnish with cilantro sprig and lime wedge.

* Tabasco-style hot sauce may be substituted.

✿ MAKES 2 CUPS

Queso Fresca Dip

2 cups queso fresca or dry small-curd cottage cheese

about 1/2 cup sweet purple onion, diced

1 green onion including green, chopped

1 medium ripe tomato, diced

1/2 cup celery, chopped

3 to 4 cloves garlic, finely minced

1 small fresh hot chile, seeded and minced, or to taste

1/4 cup fresh cilantro, minced, plus sprig for garnish

1/4 cup fresh mint leaves, minced

fresh lime juice, to taste, plus wedge for garnish

1/2 tsp crushed cumin seeds

salt and black pepper, to taste

Mix all ingredients together and put into serving dish. Garnish with cilantro sprig and lime wedge. For a quick and easy version, mix together equal parts dry small-curd cottage cheese and chunky style salsa of choice (pages 37–41).

✿ MAKES 2 CUPS

Ariba! Bean Dip

1 15 oz. can red, kidney, or pinto beans or from scratch (see Bean Tutorial, page 99)

1 medium yellow onion, diced

4 or 5 cloves garlic, finely minced

1 jalapeño chile, seeded and finely minced, to taste*

2 tsps chile powder, to taste

1 cup mayonnaise

salt and black pepper, to taste

fresh cilantro, for garnish

Drain beans, place in bowl, and mash, leaving some whole for texture. Add remaining ingredients; stir to combine and put into serving bowl. Garnish with cilantro. For a quick and delectable version, combine mashed canned beans and fresh chunky salsa. Season with salt, pepper, and hot sauce.

* Tabasco-style hot sauce may be substituted.

❀ MAKES 3 CUPS

Fun Fiesta Nachos

1 15 oz. can pinto, red, or kidney beans or from scratch

4 to 6 cloves garlic, minced

1 tbsp taco seasoning

1 tsp chile seasoning

Tabasco-style hot sauce, to taste

salt and black pepper, to taste

corn tortilla chips (commercial or see recipe, page 22)

white onion, chopped

green onion including green part, chopped

black olives, chopped

pickled jalapeño chiles, thinly sliced

chunky style salsa of choice (commercial or see page 37–41)

cheese of choice, grated

fresh cilantro, chopped, plus sprigs for ganish

sour cream

fresh lime wedges, for garnish

Preheat oven to 350 degrees. Drain beans, put into bowl. Mash well, leaving some whole for texture. Add garlic and seasonings; mix well. Line oven-proof serving dish with tortilla chips. Scatter on dollops of bean mixture, then sprinkle on onions, olives, chiles, salsa, cheese, and cilantro. Bake until cheese is melted. Remove from oven, scatter dollops of sour cream over top, and garnish with cilantro sprigs and lime wedges. Serve hot.

❀ SERVES 6 TO 10

Banditos Spiced Almonds

4 cups whole raw almonds

about 2 tbsps olive oil

1 tbsp chile powder

1 tsp garlic powder

1 tsp dried onion flakes

1 tsp sugar

Tabasco-style hot sauce, to taste

salt and black pepper, to taste

Preheat oven to 350 degrees. Mix all ingredients together well, spread on baking sheet, and bake 15–20 minutes or until almonds are hot through and are dry. Stir occasionally to make sure they bake evenly. Let cool. These are very tasty little nibbles.

✽ MAKES 4 CUPS

Deviled Eggs Puebla

12 eggs, hard-boiled, cooled, and peeled

2 to 3 cloves garlic, very finely minced

about 1/2 small yellow onion,
    very finely minced

1 green onion including green,
    finely minced

1/4 cup fresh red bell pepper, very
    finely minced

about 1/2 tsp hot chile, very finely minced,
    to taste

about 2 tbsp cilantro, very finely minced

1 tsp chile powder, to taste

juice and zest of 1 lemon, to taste

2/3 cup mayonnaise, or enough to
    moisten

salt and black pepper, to taste

Halve eggs and put yolks in bowl. Set whites aside. Mash yolks with fork. Add remaining ingredients and mix thoroughly. Adjust seasonings. Stuff whites with mixture. For special occasions top each egg with olive slice, baby shrimp, pickled pepper slice, roasted garlic clove, anchovy sliver, sardine, or a few capers. Garnish plate with fresh cilantro sprigs. These are a favorite party munchie.

✽ MAKES 24 HALVES

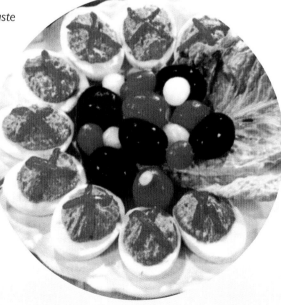

Marinated Mushrooms

1 pound fresh button mushrooms, stems removed
2 cups cider vinegar
1/4 cup olive oil
1 small onion, sliced into thin rings
6 to 8 cloves garlic, sliced thinly
1/4 cup inexpensive cream Sherry
1 tbsp cilantro, chopped
1/2 tsp cumin seeds
1 tbsp sugar
juice of 1 lemon
salt and black pepper, to taste

Blanch mushrooms and cool in cold running water. Put all remaining ingredients in saucepan; bring to boil, then remove from heat and cool. Drain mushrooms, put into jar or small crock, and pour liquid over them. Refrigerate or leave in cool dark place about 24 hours before eating.

❁ MAKES ABOUT 1 QUART

Fiesta Seafood Fondue

1 cup each cheddar and mozzarella cheese,
   grated (or Mexican equivalent)
1/4 cup cornstarch
1 cup chunky salsa, hot or mild (commercial
   or see recipe, pages 37–41)
1 cup dark full-bodied Mexican beer
   (not Guinness, Porter, or Stout)
1/4 pound imitation crabmeat, chopped
1/4 pound baby shrimp meat, chopped
dry chile flakes, to taste
1/4 cup fresh cilantro, finely chopped
salt and black pepper, to taste
flour tortillas

Toss cheeses and cornstarch together
gently. Put all ingredients into heavy pot
and cook over moderate heat until
cheese is melted, stirring gently to prevent scorching. Pour into fondue pot
and serve with wedges of soft warm
tortillas for scooping.

❀ MAKES ABOUT 4 CUPS

Seafood Ceviche

1 pound firm-flesh white fish fillets
1/2 pound small raw shrimp
1/2 pound small scallops
1 sweet purple onion, sliced into thin rings
2 green onions including green, chopped
1 large ripe tomato, diced
1 Anaheim or poblano chile, roasted
1 jalapeño chile, seeded and sliced
   into very thin rings
1/4 cup chopped cilantro
3 tbsps olive oil
1 tbsp sugar
juice of 4 to 6 limes
salt and black pepper to taste
crisp lettuce
avocado slices, for garnish
tomato slices, for garnish

Cut fish into bite-size chunks. Peel
shrimp. Cut scallops in half. Put
seafood into colander and rinse
well under cold running water. Pat
dry and put into large bowl. Add
remaining ingredients and stir gently.
Refrigerate at least 3–4 hours before
serving. Pile onto bed of lettuce and
garnish with avocado and tomato slices.

❀ MAKES ABOUT 6 CUPS

Fiesta Empanadas

pastry (see recipe to right)

beef filling (see
    recipe to right)

1 egg

1 tbsp water

Preheat oven to
500 degrees.
Remove pastry from
refrigerator and roll to pie
crust thickness, a little less than 1/4
inch. Using large biscuit cutter or
glass, cut pastry into 2 1/2- to 3-inch
circles. Put scant tablespoon cooled
filling into center of each circle, being
careful not to get any on outside
edge. Beat egg and water together;
paint outer rim lightly with egg wash.
Fold circle in half and crimp shut
using fork tines. Line baking sheet
with baker's parchment. Place
empanadas about 1 inch apart on
parchment. Paint surface with egg
wash; bake 5 minutes. Reduce heat to
350 degrees; bake 20–25 minutes or
until golden brown. Serve while hot
or cool completely.

Pastry

5 cups all-purpose flour

1 pound butter, margarine,
    shortening, or lard
        (4 sticks or 2 cups)

1 large egg

1 tbsp white vinegar

To make pastry: Put flour into
large bowl; cut butter into flour with
wire pastry blender until the texture
of coarse cornmeal. Put egg and vinegar into 1-cup measure; mix with fork.
Add 1 cup of cold water to flour mixture; stir with fork until a rough ball is
formed. Turn onto lightly floured surface and knead very gently — just
shoving the pastry together — into a
ball. (Do not overwork. Overworking
pastry makes it very tough.) Cut pastry in half and form into two disks,
about 6 inches in diameter. Wrap in
plastic and refrigerate about 30 minutes. Although this pastry may be
frozen, it is better if used fresh.

❀ MAKES FOUR 8- TO 9-INCH CRUSTS WITH
   ENOUGH DOUGH LEFT OVER FOR DECORATIONS.

Beef Filling

1 pound ground beef

2 tbsps olive oil

1 medium yellow onion, chopped

6 to 8 cloves garlic, minced

1/2 stalk celery, chopped

1/2 red bell pepper, chopped

2 tomatoes, chopped

1 small hot chile, seeded and minced,
    to taste

1 tsp Italian seasoning

1 tsp chile seasoning

1 tbsp sugar

2 tbsps red wine vinegar

1 cup beef stock, broth, or bouillon

salt and black pepper, to taste

To make filling: Lightly sauté beef in
heavy skillet, breaking beef into small
pieces and leaving a bit of pink. Strain
beef. Because empanadas will be
eaten cold, run beef under hot water
to remove any fat. Drain; set aside.
Wipe skillet; add oil. Gently sauté
onion and garlic until soft and pinkish
but not beginning to brown. Add celery, pepper, tomatoes, and chile; continue to sauté a few more minutes.
Add remaining ingredients except salt
and pepper. Return beef to pan, stir

well, cover, reduce heat to simmer, and cook 15–20 minutes, stirring occasionally. Remove cover; add salt and pepper. If mixture is still wet, remove cover and simmer a while longer to reduce liquid. Remove from stove and allow to cool thoroughly before assembling empanadas.

Bean Filling

about 2 cups canned or cooked pinto
    beans, mashed (see Bean Tutorial,
    page 99)
1 cup salsa (commercial or see
    recipe, pages 3–41)
salt and black pepper, to taste

To make filling: Mix together and season with salt and pepper.

Chicken Filling

2 cups cooked chicken, chopped
1 cup Salsa Verde (commercial or see
    recipe, page 41)

To make filling: Mix together well. Fill and bake as directed on beef filling recipe.

Pork Filling

1 pound ground pork or sausage
1 large yellow onion, diced
4 to 6 cloves garlic, minced
1 cup Salsa Verde (commercial or
    see recipe, page 41)
1/4 cup fresh cilantro, chopped
salt, black pepper, and dry chile flakes,
    to taste

To make filling: Heat heavy skillet; lightly sauté meat 2–3 minutes, breaking meat into small pieces. Sauté until meat begins to brown and releases some fat. Drain most of the fat; add onion and garlic. Continue to sauté until onion is soft, pinkish, and translucent but not yet browned. Stir in Salsa Verde. Add cilantro; season with salt, pepper, and chile flakes. Cool mixture completely. Fill and bake as above.

Chorizo and Bean Filling

about 1/2 pound chorizo
1 large onion, diced
4 to 6 cloves garlic, minced
1 stalk celery, diced
1 sweet red pepper, seeded and diced
fresh hot chiles, seeded and finely minced,
    to taste
2 cups cooked beans, mashed (commercial
    or see Bean Tutorial, page 99)
1 cup salsa (commercial or see recipes
    page 37–41)
1/2 cup fresh cilantro, chopped

To make filling: Sauté chorizo in heavy skillet. Drain most of the fat, add onion and garlic, and continue to sauté until soft and translucent but not yet beginning to brown. Add celery, pepper, and chiles; continue to sauté until soft and just beginning to brown. Add beans; mix thoroughly, and sauté 2–3 minutes, breaking beans if they begin to form a crust. Add salsa and cilantro, mix well, and cool thoroughly. Fill and bake as above.

> **Other ideas:** Egg salad filling
> Tuna salad filling

Basic Taquitos

24 corn tortillas 4 or 5 inches in diameter

olive oil or melted lard

about 1 cup refried beans blended
   until smooth

favorite cheese, cut into thin slivers a
   bit shorter than tortillas are wide

about 2 cups cooked beef, pork, or chicken,
   finely chopped and seasoned to taste

Soften tortillas by lightly frying one at a time in oil until soft but not brown or crisp. Spread beans thinly on tortilla. Lay one sliver of cheese at one end of tortilla. Add thin line of meat. Roll tortilla as tightly as possible — the diameter of a cigarillo, not a fat stogy. Set aside on flat dish, seam side down. Fill and roll all tortillas. Heat about 1/2 inch oil to frying temperature. Fry several tortillas at a time until crisp and nicely browned on both sides, turning with tongs. Place on paper towels to drain. Serve warm with Glorious Guacamole (see recipe page 24) for dipping.

❋ MAKES ABOUT 24

Corn and Pepper Fritters

1 cup (masa) harina

1/2 cup all-purpose flour

1/2 cup yellow cornmeal

1 tbsp baking powder

1 tbsp chile powder

1 cup corn kernels, fresh or frozen

1 medium onion, diced

4 to 6 cloves garlic, minced

1 sweet red bell pepper, seeded and diced

dry chile flakes, to taste

1/2 cup fresh cilantro, chopped

3 eggs, lightly beaten

1/4 cup olive oil, plus additional for frying

about 1 1/2 cups water, or enough to
   make a very stiff batter

salt and black pepper, to taste

Mix together all ingredients except oil for frying. Heat about 1/8 inch oil in heavy skillet; drop batter by tablespoons into skillet. Fry over moderate heat until lightly browned on one side. Turn; fry 2–3 minutes until done. Test one for doneness. Excellent served by themselves or topped with salsa and sour cream.

❋ MAKES ABOUT 24

Fiesta Surprise (Masa) Balls

2 cups (masa) harina

1 tbsp chile powder, or more to taste

dry chile flakes, to taste

1/2 tsp cumin seeds, crushed

1/4 cup fresh cilantro, chopped

salt and black pepper, to taste

about 1 1/2 cups water

2 tbsps olive oil

about 24 1/2-inch cubes of mozzarella
    cheese or Mexican equivalent

fresh cilanatro sprigs, for garnish

Mix all dry ingredients together; begin
adding water slowly, stirring well after each
addition, to form dough. To test for seasoning,
heat a bit of oil in heavy skillet, form a bit of
dough into flat pancake, and fry gently on both sides.
Taste and adjust seasonings. Cover dough with plastic
wrap and let sit about 30 minutes. Cut cheese into 1/2-inch
cubes. Heat oil in heavy pot to deep-frying temperature, about 360 degrees.
Pinch off walnut-size piece of dough, form into ball, and push cheese cube
inside. Pinch dough to seal; reform into ball. Continue with remaining dough
and cheese. Gently drop one ball into hot oil and deep fry until golden
brown on all sides. Remove and drain on paper towels. When cool enough to
handle, test for doneness. Cheese should pull into strings when you bite into
ball. Be careful not to burn your tongue! Continue with remaining balls.
Garnish with fresh cilantro sprigs. Serve hot with salsa for dipping, if desired.

🌸 MAKES ABOUT 24 DEPENDING ON SIZE

33

Apris

Apris are a delightful little bit of something, not difficult to make and very useful when you're giving a party. They are little disks of (masa) harina, lightly fried and used as a base for tasty toppings. They make excellent appetizers and snacks. Make them ahead, even freeze them and then thaw, lightly toast in the oven or heat in a microwave, place on a serving platter, and top with all sorts delicious goodies. Toppings may be as simple as dollops of salsa or guacamole and a bit of sour cream, or as exotic as a grilled shrimp, barbecued meat, ceviche, or olive paste. See following recipes for ideas.

2 1/2 cups masa harina

1/4 cup olive oil or melted lard

1 tbsp baking powder

salt, to taste

about 2 cups water, or enough to make pliable dough

olive oil for frying

Mix all ingredients except oil for frying together until pliable dough is formed. Cover with plastic wrap; let sit about 30 minutes. Pinch off walnut-size pieces of dough and form into disks about 1/2-inch thick. Press your thumb into the center of each disk to hold toppings — as if you are making upside-down sombreros. As you make them, place them on a plate and cover with plastic wrap so they won't dry out. Pan fry or deep fry them.

To pan fry: heat about 1/4 inch oil in heavy skillet. Do test run with one or two apris. Put several into skillet and fry gently on both sides, 2–3 minutes total, until light golden brown. Drain on paper towels. Continue with remaining apris. When drained, they are ready for toppings.

To deep fry: heat several inches oil in suitable pot or fryer to deep-frying temperature, about 360 degrees. Gently drop one in for test run. Slide several into oil; fry 2–3 minutes total, only until light golden brown. (Overfrying will make them hard.) Remove from oil with slotted spoon; drain on paper towels. Continue with remaining apris. When drained, they are ready for toppings.

❋ MAKES ABOUT 3 OR 4 DOZEN DEPENDING ON SIZE

Cheese and Salsa Apris

Preheat oven to 350 degrees. Place apris on baking sheet; put a dollop of salsa on each. Top with grated cheese; bake until cheese melts. Serve hot.

Avocado and Shrimp Apris

1 large ripe avocado, diced very small

1 cup baby shrimp meat, diced very small

1/2 cup fresh salsa of choice, drained

Mix together well and place a dollop on each apris.

Roasted Garlic and Clam Apris

1 6 1/2-oz. can minced or chopped clams, drained

1/2 cup sour cream

6 to 8 cloves roasted garlic, minced (commercial or see recipe, page 45)

2 tbsps fresh cilantro, minced

salt and black pepper, to taste

Mix all ingredients together well and place a generous dollop on each apris.

Zesty Bean Apris

1 cup refried beans (commercial or see Bean Tutorial, page 99)

1 canned chipotle chile, finely minced, to taste

1/4 cup fresh cilantro, minced

salt and black pepper, to taste

grated cheese

small fresh cilantro sprigs, for garnish

Preheat oven or broiler to 350 degrees. Mix beans, chile, cilantro, salt, and pepper together well. Place apris on baking sheet; top each with generous dollop of mixture. Top with grated cheese; put in oven just until cheese begins to melt. Garnish each with cilantro sprig; serve hot.

Salsas y Mas

Salsas & More

Basic Salsa Fresca Rojo

This is a good basic red salsa fresca. Add or remove ingredients depending on their availability and your family's tastes.

6 to 8 large tomatoes, chopped
2 large yellow onions, chopped
4 to 6 green onions including green, chopped
8 to 10 cloves garlic, finely minced
1 large red bell pepper, seeded and chopped
1 large yellow bell pepper, seeded and chopped
2 Anaheim or poblano chiles, seeded and chopped
3 to 4 small hot chiles of choice, seeded and finely minced, to taste
1 stalk celery, chopped very small
1/2 cup cilantro, chopped
1/4 cup fresh parsley, finely chopped
2 tbsps fresh dill weed, finely chopped
1 tbsp fresh Mexican oregano, finely minced
1/2 tsp cumin
3 tbsps sugar
1 tsp black pepper
juice of 3 to 4 limes
salt, to taste

Mix all ingredients together well and refrigerate in covered container. Salsa will last at least two weeks refrigerated.

✿ MAKES ABOUT 4 CUPS

San Joaquin Salsa Crudo

4 large ripe tomatoes, chopped
2 yellow onions, chopped
6 to 8 jalapeño or other hot chiles, seeded and minced very small, to taste
10 cloves garlic, minced very small
1/4 cup fresh cilantro, chopped
1 tbsp fresh Mexican oregano, chopped, or 1/2 tsp dry
1/2 tsp cumin
1 cup tomato ketchup (yep, you heard me, tomato ketchup)
juice and zest of 1 lemon
salt and black pepper, to taste

Mix all ingredients together well and store in refrigerator overnight before using.

✿ MAKES ABOUT 1 QUART

No Wimps Allowed! Salsa

Hold onto your hats! This salsa is armed and dangerous. Only charter members of the galvanized gullet should try this one.

1 large yellow onion, chopped

3 green onions, including green, chopped

6 to 8 cloves garlic, finely minced

1 red bell pepper, seeded and chopped

2 Anaheim chiles, seeded and chopped

4 to 6 jalapeño chiles, seeded and minced

4 to 6 serrano chiles, seeded and minced

2 to 4 habañero chiles, seeded and minced

3 tomatoes, chopped, plus 3 tomatoes, puréed

4 tomatillos, chopped

1/2 cup fresh cilantro, chopped

1/4 cup fresh lime juice, to taste

3 tbsps sugar, to taste

salt and black pepper, to taste

Mix all ingredients together and refrigerate several hours before using. Salsa will last at least one week refrigerated.

✸ MAKES ABOUT 3 TO 4 CUPS

Grilled Chipotle and Tomato Salsa Roja

6 ripe tomatoes, cut in half

1 cup onions, sliced

4 jalapeño chiles, seeded and sliced

4 garlic cloves, chopped

olive oil

2 tbsps chipotle chile purée

2 green onions including green part, finely chopped

1/2 cup fresh cilantro leaves, chopped

1/2 cup fresh lime juice

sugar,* salt, and black pepper, to taste

Place tomatoes, onions, chiles, and garlic on baking sheet; brush with olive oil. Broil until tomato skins begin to blacken and are a bit soft. Turn ingredients once or twice during blackening. Remove and let cool. Process in blender or food processor to coarse purée. Remove to bowl and add remaining ingredients. Adjust seasonings. Refrigerate until ready to use.

* Yes, sugar. Many find that the addition of a bit of sugar enhances the rich smoky flavors. Experiment. Add just a wee bit at a time until it suits your taste.

❀ MAKES ABOUT 4 CUPS

Roasted Tomatillo Salsa Verde

10 to 12 tomatillos

1 to 2 yellow onions

2 to 3 tbsps olive oil

1 green bell pepper, roasted (see directions, page 45, for roasting all chiles)

3 to 4 Anaheim chiles, roasted

2 to 3 jalapeño chiles, roasted, to taste

10 to 12 cloves garlic, roasted (see directions page 45)

1/4 cup fresh cilantro, chopped

1/4 cup fresh lime juice

1 tsp fresh Mexican oregano, minced (or favorite fresh herbs)

1/2 tsp cumin seeds, crushed

1 tbsp sugar

salt and black pepper, to taste

Preheat oven to 350 degrees. Husk and wash tomatillos and put on baking sheet. Cut onions into thick slices and put on same baking sheet. Brush with oil. Bake until slightly soft and starting to brown, about 15 to 20 minutes, but keep watching them. Remove and let cool. Chop pepper and chiles coarsely. Put all ingredients into blender or food processor; process to desired texture. Adjust seasonings. Let sit at least 1 hour before using.

❀ MAKES 2 TO 3 CUPS

Tropical Fruit Salsa

This sweet salsa is delicious as a condiment with pork, chicken, and seafood. It also makes a nice salad. Put a scoop on a lettuce leaf and garnish with fresh orange and avocado slices.

1 cup fresh pineapple, diced
2 mangos, peeled and diced
1 papaya, peeled, seeded, and chopped
1 seedless orange, peeled and diced
1/2 cup sweet purple onion, chopped
1 serrano chile, seeded and minced, to taste
1/4 cup fresh cilantro, minced
1/4 cup fresh mint leaves, minced
1 tsp fresh ginger root, finely grated
2 to 3 tbsps sugar, to taste
black pepper, to taste

Mix all ingredients together. Let sit at least 1 hour before serving.

✿ MAKES 3 TO 4 CUPS

Salsa Verde

2 Anaheim or long roasting chiles

1 or more small hot green chiles of choice, to taste

10 to 12 tomatillos

3 tbsps olive oil

2 large yellow onions, diced

3 to 4 green onions including green, chopped

10 to 12 cloves garlic

2 stalks celery, chopped

1 large green bell pepper, seeded and chopped

1 tsp Mexican oregano

1/2 tsp cumin

1/2 cup fresh cilantro, chopped

2 tbsps sugar

juice of 6 limes (about 1/2 cup)

4 cups chicken stock, broth, or bouillon

salt and black pepper, to taste

Roast chiles and tomatillos until skins are blistered. Rub off chile skins under cold running water; remove seeds. Chop chiles and tomatillos; set aside. Heat olive oil in large heavy skillet; gently sauté onions, garlic, celery, and pepper until soft and just beginning to brown around edges. Add chiles, tomatillos, oregano, cumin, and cilantro. Gently sauté 2–3 minutes. Add sugar, lime juice, stock, and salt and pepper. Stir; bring to gentle boil. Reduce heat to simmer; continue cooking until salsa is reduced to thick sauce, stirring periodically to prevent scorching. For smoother texture, process in blender or food processor.

Excellent with chicken or pork, in chicken enchiladas and some seafood dishes; great with grilled vegetable tacos and burritos or just as a dip or a topping for bean and rice dishes.

❁ MAKES ABOUT 3 TO 4 CUPS

Basic Adobo Sauce

10 to 12 canned chipotle chiles, chopped

2 large yellow onions, diced

12 cloves garlic, chopped

4 to 6 tomatoes, diced

4 tbsps tomato paste

1 tsp Mexican oregano

1/2 tsp ground cumin

1/2 tsp cumin seeds

1/4 cup sugar

1/2 cup cider vinegar

1/2 cup fresh cilantro, chopped

4 cups water

Put all ingredients into pot, bring to boil, reduce heat to simmer, and cook until liquid is reduced by half. Cool; process in blender until smooth. Refrigerate in jar with tight-fitting lid.

❀ MAKES ABOUT 2 CUPS

Vegetarian and Vegan Chile Sauce

about 6 dried ancho or poblano chiles

1 cup boiling water

2 to 3 tbsps olive oil

1 yellow onion, diced

6 to 8 cloves garlic, chopped

1 bell pepper, seeded and chopped

1 stalk of celery, chopped

jalapeño chiles, seeded and minced, to taste

3 to 4 tomatoes, chopped

1 tbsp Italian seasoning

1 tsp cumin seeds

1 tsp cinnamon

1 tsp fresh ginger root, grated

2 to 3 tbsps sugar, to taste

1/4 cup cider vinegar, to taste

vegetable stock, enough to form a rich sauce (see recipe, page 47)

salt and black pepper, to taste

Put dried chiles in bowl and add enough boiling water to cover. Let sit 15-20 minutes. Remove, reserving water, and remove stem and seeds. Set chiles aside. Heat oil in heavy skillet; gently sauté onion and garlic until soft and just beginning to brown around edges. Add celery, pepper, and jalapeño chiles; continue to sauté until soft. Add tomatoes, seasonings, and vinegar. Chop dried chiles and add to the sauce. Simmer until all vegetables are soft. Add about 1/2 cup soaking water and enough stock to make sauce, about 2 to 3 cups. Bring to boil, reduce heat, and simmer 20-30 minutes. You may need to add more stock. Season with salt and pepper, perhaps bit more sugar and vinegar. When vegetables are quite soft, remove from heat and let cool a bit. Process to smooth sauce in blender or food processor. If it seems too thin, return to the pan and continue to simmer until it thickens, stirring frequently to prevent scorching.

❀ MAKES 3 TO 4 CUPS

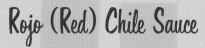

Rojo (Red) Chile Sauce

This is a good basic cooked red sauce to use when making enchiladas, stews, or for cooking meats.

2 to 3 tbsps olive oil or lard

1 large yellow onion, chopped

8 to 10 cloves garlic, chopped

3 to 4 Anaheim or similar mild chiles, seeded and chopped

2 jalapeño chiles, seeded and chopped, to taste

3 or 4 tomatoes, chopped

2 to 3 tomatillos, chopped

1 tbsp Mexican oregano, or herbs of choice

1 tsp cinnamon

1/2 tsp ground cloves

1 tsp fresh ginger root, grated

1 tsp cumin seeds

2 to 3 tbsps sugar, to taste

1/4 cup red wine vinegar, to taste

3 tbsps tomato paste

3 cups broth, stock, or bouillon (see recipe, page 47)

salt and black pepper, to taste

Heat olive oil in heavy skillet and gently sauté onion and garlic. Add all ingredients except tomato paste, broth, and salt and pepper; continue to sauté several minutes or until vegetables are softening. Whisk tomato paste into stock and add. Stir well and simmer, stirring occasionally, about 10 minutes. Cool slightly; process in blender or food processor until smooth. Season with salt and pepper. If sauce is too thin, return to skillet and simmer until desired thickness is reached.

❀ MAKES 3 TO 4 CUPS

Ancho Mayonnaise Sauce

NOTE: This recipe contains a raw egg.

4 dried ancho chiles, canned chipotle chiles,
  or other favorite chiles
boiling water
1 raw egg
6 cloves garlic
1/2 tsp dry mustard
1/2 tsp sugar
2 tsps sugar
juice of 1 lemon
2 1/2 cups vegetable oil

Remove chile seeds. Put chiles in bowl and cover with boiling water. Let sit about 20 minutes. Remove, reserving water, and put into blender. Crush garlic cloves and add to blender. Add 2–3 tablespoons reserved water; process to smooth paste. Strain through sieve to remove small chunks; discard. Put paste into bowl and add all remaining ingredients except oil. With a handheld beater blend until thick and creamy. Add oil very slowly, no more than 1 tablespoon at a time, incorporating thoroughly after each addition. After using about half the oil, mixture will thicken. Begin adding oil about 1/4 cup at a time, always incorporating thoroughly after each addition. When all oil is used, taste and adjust seasonings. Mayonnaise will keep in refrigerator at least one month.

✿ MAKES ABOUT 2 1/2 CUPS

Techniques

Roasting Garlic

Peel garlic cloves. Lightly wipe a heavy skillet with olive oil. Add cloves in a single layer. Roast slowly over low heat. Flip cloves frequently to ensure even roasting. When cloves are pale golden brown and soft when pressure is applied, they are done, 30–40 minutes.

Roasted garlic is a wonderful addition to many dishes. It has an almost sweet, nutlike flavor — wonderful in many dishes or just lightly salted and munched on.

Peeled garlic is available in 8-ounce and 1-pound jars. Be sure to buy whole peeled cloves, not chopped garlic.

Roasting Chiles and Peppers

Oven roasting: Bake chiles at about 400 degrees on a baking sheet until skins are blistered. Remove skins under cold running water. Although oven roasting is the easier way, I think flame roasting is better. Oven roasting doesn't develop quite as much flavor as flame roasting does, and although the skins are blistering, the chiles are cooking, too. You may want softened chiles for some dishes. However, in many applications chiles should retain a firmer texture. For these applications I prefer flame roasting.

Flame or direct heat roasting: Use a barbeque or a stovetop burner – electric or gas. Lay chiles directly over the heat and with a pair of tongs turn them frequently to ensure the skins blister evenly. When skins are blistered, immediately wrap chiles in a cloth or put them in a brown paper bag. Let steam 3–4 minutes in the bag before removing skins under cold running water. Flame-roasted chiles still have good texture and are excellent for using in salads, for putting in vinaigrettes, and as appetizers.

Choose chiles that have the fewest convolutions. If they are too twisted and bumpy, it is difficult to blister the skins evenly. Don't roast more chiles than you can peel before they become completely cold. Cold skin is very hard to remove. Don't worry about removing every smidgen of charred skin. A bit of char is what gives the characteristic roasted chile flavor.

Sopas y Ensaladas
Soups & Salads

Basic Instructions for Stock, Broth, or Bouillon

The most important item to have in your larder at all times is an ample supply of stock, broth, or bouillon. What's the difference? Stock usually refers to homemade broth; broth is a canned product; and bouillon is powder or concentrated cubes. They are all made by cooking together bits and pieces of animal, bone, or vegetable, and often all three, until they produce a flavorful liquid used for soup or as a liquid that adds flavor to other foods. You may use commercial broth or bouillon in all the recipes. However, stock isn't hard to make.

Basic Stock

To make meat, poultry, or fish stock, begin with uncooked bones and scraps of meat, use bones and scraps you have already cooked, or use a combination. If you use raw bones and scraps, you may want to caramelize them first. Put a bit of oil or fat in a heavy pot, add the bones and scraps, and sear them on all sides until they are nicely browned. Browning carmelizes the natural sugars, thus developing the flavor.

Usually, the only time I caramelize is when I am making vegetable stock because the vegetables need a bit more help.

Put meat, poultry, or fish scraps, cooked or uncooked, in a large pot. Add an onion or two. Don't bother to peel or chop it; just quarter it. The peel will add color to the stock. Add a bulb of garlic. Again, don't bother to peel, just cut it in half. Add a tablespoon of Italian seasoning or sprigs of your favorite fresh herbs. Add vegetable peels and scraps or tired vegetables from the refrigerator. (Do not, however, use beets. They will turn your stock a nasty color.) Cover everything with cold water, bring to a boil, then lower the heat to maintain a simmer, cover with a tight-fitting lid, and continue to cook for an hour or two. Strain. To defat strained stock, allow it to cool completely. The fat will solidify and float to the top. Remove it. If the fat is not firm enough to remove easily, refrigerate before defatting.

Even after straining, stock will have some small bits and pieces in it. Usually, that doesn't matter. However, occasionally you may need a perfectly clear stock, and you'll need to clarify it. Cool the stock completely. Beat an egg or two and whisk into the cold stock. Turn the heat very low and gradually heat the stock. Do not stir. When the stock has heated, the eggs will have cooked and risen to the surface, bringing the pieces with them. Strain the stock again through a clean cloth. Occasionally, you may to repeat these steps to get a perfectly clear stock.

Vegetable Stock

Heat a bit of olive oil in a heavy pot and brown a chopped onion or two and at least a dozen cloves of garlic – the more the better. Add a chopped bell pepper, two or three chopped celery stalks, other veggies such as carrots, cabbage, potatoes, leeks, or green onions, and continue to sauté until all are lightly browned and softened. Add enough water to stand 3 to 4 inches over the surface of the veggies. Add sprigs of whatever herbs you like and bring to a boil. Reduce the heat to maintain a simmer, cover with a tight-fitting lid, and simmer about an hour. Strain and season to taste with salt and pepper.

Storing Stock

I always like to have stock on hand. It will last for about a week in the refrigerator. Otherwise, put it into ice cube trays and freeze, then put the frozen cubes into resealable plastic bags. You'll always have them readily available no matter how much or how little you need. One or two "flavor cubes" added to a stir fry, sautéed veggies, pasta, or rice can be a great enhancement. It's instant flavor at your fingertips.

Harvest Fiesta Soup

2 tbsps olive oil

1 onion, diced

6 to 8 cloves garlic, sliced thinly

1/4 pound lean beef, cut into thin strips 1/2 inch wide, 2 inches long, paper thin

2 quarts beef stock, broth, or bouillon (commercial or see recipe, page 47)

1 tbsp Italian seasoning or favorite fresh herbs, to taste

1/4 cup pearl barley

1/4 cup lentils

1 cup red, kidney, or pinto beans, cooked

2 to 3 cups assorted blanched vegetables such as carrots, potatoes, green beans, parsnip, and pumpkin, cut into bite-size chunks

1/2 cup fresh or frozen corn kernels (do not blanch)

1 small zucchini, sliced (do not blanch)

1 red bell pepper, seeded and cut into julienne

1 small jalapeño chile, seeded and cut into thin rings (optional)

salt and black pepper, to taste

1/4 cup fresh parsley or cilantro, chopped

Put oil in large heavy pot and gently sauté onion and garlic. Add beef and sauté until just beginning to brown around edges. Add stock, Italian seasoning, barley, and lentils; simmer for about 45 to 60 minutes, until the barley and lentils are done. Add beans, vegetables, and chile; simmer until vegetables reach desired degree of doneness. I prefer my vegetables to still have some crunch to them. Season with salt and pepper; stir in parsley.

To really give this soup the fiesta flair, serve it in a hollowed-out pumpkin shell. Fill the shell with hot water and let it sit for several minutes; otherwise, the pumpkin will cool the soup. Then toss the water. Stabilize the pumpkin by setting it in a wok ring, or wet a clean tea towel with warm water, ring it out, and twist it into a donut shape. Set the pumpkin in it. Use greenery, flowers, fruit, or vegetables to hide the holder and make a festive presentation.

❀ SERVES 6 TO 8 AS MAIN COURSE, MORE AS FIRST COURSE

Zesty Meatball Soup

1 to 2 tbsps olive oil

1 large yellow onion, chopped

6 to 8 cloves garlic, chopped

1 serrano chile, seeded and minced, to taste

8 cups beef stock, broth, or bouillon (commercial or
   see recipe, page 47)

1 tbsp Italian seasoning

1 tbsp chile powder

1 red bell pepper, seeded and julienned

1 Anaheim chile, seeded and cut into thin rings

2 tomatoes, chopped

kernels from 2 ears of corn

1 or 2 small zucchini, sliced

salt and black pepper, to taste

meatballs (see recipe to right)

1/4 cup fresh cilantro, chopped

Heat oil in heavy pot and gently sauté onion, garlic, and
chile until just beginning to brown. Add stock, Italian seasoning, and chile powder, bring to boil, and immediately
reduce to simmer; cook 20–30 minutes. Add remaining
ingredients except meatballs and cilantro; continue
simmering until vegetables reach desired degree of doneness. Season with salt and pepper. Put meatballs in serving
dish and pour soup over them. Sprinkle lightly with
cilantro. This is an excellent and satisfying meal in a bowl.

Meatballs:

8 tbsps olive oil, divided

1 yellow onion, chopped small

6 to 8 cloves garlic, minced

1 small serrano chile, seeded and minced, to taste

about 1 pound pork, ground

about 1 pound beef, ground

1 tbsp chile powder, to taste

1/4 cup fresh cilantro, minced

2 eggs

salt and black pepper, to taste

To make meatballs:

Heat 1–2 tablespoons oil in heavy skillet and gently sauté
onion, garlic, and chile until soft and translucent. Cool.
Put into bowl with remaining ingredients. Mix thoroughly.
Make one small meat patty and sauté in skillet until done
to test for seasonings. Adjust seasonings. Form into walnut-
size meatballs. Put remaining 2–3 tablespoons oil in skillet;
gently sauté meatballs until just cooked through. Do not
overcook.

❄ SERVES 6 TO 8 AS MAIN COURSE, MORE AS FIRST COURSE

Tortilla Ball Soup

2 to 3 tbsps olive oil or lard

1 onion, chopped

4 to 6 cloves garlic, chopped

1 tsp oregano

1/2 tbsp chile powder

4 to 6 ripe tomatoes, diced

8 cups chicken stock, broth, or bouillon,
(commercial or see recipe, page 47)

1/4 cup fresh cilantro, chopped

salt and black pepper, to taste

dried chile flakes, to taste

tortilla balls (see recipe to right)

Tortilla balls:

12 to 16 corn tortillas (depending on size)

1 cup warm milk

1/2 cup queso aqejo, finely grated
(or Romano or Parmesan cheese)

1 to 2 eggs, beaten

2 tbsps cilantro, finely minced

salt and pepper, to taste

olive oil or lard

Heat oil in heavy skillet and sauté onion and garlic until lightly caramelized. Add oregano, chile powder, and tomatoes and continue to cook about 5 minutes. Let cool slightly, then purée in blender or food processor until smooth. Pour into large pot and add stock. Just before serving add chile flakes and tortilla balls; simmer until heated thoroughly.

Break tortillas into small pieces and process into crumbs. Add remaining ingredients except oil; knead dough in processor or by hand. Cover with plastic wrap and refrigerate several hours or overnight to allow tortillas to soften and dough to become malleable. Divide dough into 24 equal pieces and form into small balls. Heat oil in heavy skillet and fry balls until golden brown on all sides. Drain well and set aside.

❄ SERVES 6 TO 8 AS MAIN COURSE,
MORE AS FIRST COURSE

Fresh Corn and Roasted Chile Soup

2 to 3 tbsps olive oil or lard

1 onion, chopped

4 to 6 cloves garlic, minced

4 or 5 ripe tomatoes, diced

1 tsp oregano

1/2 tsp cumin seeds, crushed

1 red sweet bell pepper, roasted,
(see instructions, page 45), seeded,
and julienned

2 Anaheim chiles, roasted (see instructions
page 45), seeded, and coarsely chopped

about 3 cups corn kernels, cut fresh
from ears or frozen

8 cups chicken stock, broth, or bouillon
(commercial or see recipe, page 47)

salt and black pepper, to taste

1/4 cup fresh cilantro, chopped

queso fresco or ricotta cheese, crumbled

Heat oil in pot and sauté onion and garlic until soft and lightly browned. Add tomatoes, oregano, and cumin; continue to sauté until tomatoes begin to release some juice, 3–4 minutes. Add pepper, chiles, and corn; continue to sauté 2–3 minutes. Add stock and heat through. Season with salt and pepper; stir in cilantro. Serve in individual bowls accompanied by queso fresco to sprinkle over. Salsa often accompanies this soup.

❀ SERVES 6 TO 8 AS MAIN COURSE,
MORE AS FIRST COURSE

54

Cream of Pumpkin Soup

2 tbsps olive oil

1 medium yellow onion, diced

4 to 6 cloves garlic, minced

1 1/2 cups canned pumpkin

6 cups chicken stock, broth, or bouillon
(commercial or see recipe, page 47)

1 tbsp fresh or 1 tsp dry dill weed, minced
plus sprigs for garnish

1/2 tsp ground nutmeg

1/2 cup inexpensive cream Sherry

2 cups heavy cream

salt and black pepper, to taste

sour cream, for garnish

Heat oil in heavy skillet and gently sauté onion and garlic until soft and translucent but not beginning to brown. Add pumpkin and cook 2–3 minutes, stirring frequently to prevent scorching. Allow to cool slightly for safety; process into smooth puree in blender or food processor. Add a bit of stock to process, if needed. Pour pumpkin mixture into pot and add remaining stock and dill weed. Bring to brisk simmer, whisking constantly. Add Sherry and cream; continue whisking until hot through. Do not allow to boil. Season with salt and pepper. To serve, garnish each serving with dollop of sour cream and dill weed sprig. This soup is simple and delicious, particularly festive if served in a hollowed-out pumpkin shell (see recipe for Harvest Fiesta Soup page 49).

❀ SERVES 6 TO 8 AS MAIN
   COURSE, MORE AS
   FIRST COURSE

Cream of Avocado Soup

1 pint heavy cream or whipping cream

4 large very ripe avocados, mashed, plus
   slices for garnish

6 cups chicken broth, stock, or bouillon
   (commercial or see recipe, page 47)

1/4 to 1/2 cup inexpensive
   cream Sherry, to taste

grating of nutmeg

salt and black pepper,
   to taste

lime slices for garnish

Put cream and avocados in blender and process. Put cream mixture and stock in pot. Cook over low heat until hot, whisking occasionally to prevent scorching. Add Sherry and nutmeg; whisk. Season with salt and pepper; garnish with avocado and lime slices. This soup is excellent served hot or chilled.

❀ SERVES 6 TO 8 AS MAIN COURSE,
   MORE AS FIRST COURSE

Chilled Seafood Soup

8 cups chicken stock, broth, or bouillon
   (commercial or see recipe, page 47)

1 small sweet purple onion, 1/2 cut into thin rings,
   1/2 diced

6 cloves garlic, minced

2 green onions including green part, chopped small

1 red bell pepper, seeded and julienned

1 Anaheim chile, seeded and cut into thin rings

1 jalapeno chile, seeded and very finely minced

1 small cucumber, about 2/3 diced and
   1/3 cut into thin rings

2 tomatoes, diced

2 avocados, diced

1/4 cup fresh cilantro, chopped

1/2 cup cream Sherry

1/2 pound each cooked baby shrimpmeat
   and crabmeat

salt and black pepper, to taste

This one is easy! Combine all ingredients
except diced onion and cucumber rings in
large bowl. Season with salt and pepper.
Float diced onion and cucumber rings on top
and serve ice cold on a hot, hot day.

❀ SERVES 6 TO 8 AS MAIN COURSE,
   MORE AS FIRST COURSE

Gazpacho

1 49 oz. can tomato juice
4 cups chicken stock, broth, or bouillon
    (commercial or see recipe, page 47)
1/2 cup inexpensive cream Sherry
1 cup salsa (commercial or see recipe, page 37)
2 avocados, diced
2 tomatoes, diced
1 medium green onion, about 2/3 diced
    and 1/3 cut into thin rings
1 medium cucumber, about 1/4 diced
    and 3/4 cut into thin rings
1/4 cup black olives, sliced
2 tbsps capers
jalapeño chiles, seeded and sliced into thin rings, to taste
1/4 cup fresh cilantro, chopped, plus sprigs for garnish
1/4 cup fresh dill weed, chopped, plus sprigs for garnish
salt and black pepper, to taste
several slices lemon, skin on

Combine all ingredients except onion rings, cucumber rings, and lemon slices; chill thoroughly. Serve in large bowl with large chunk of ice in it. Float onion rings, cucumber rings, and lemon slices on top; garnish with fresh cilantro and dill weed sprigs. This is delicious on a hot day and a wonderful fiesta dish.

❀ SERVES 8 TO 10 OR MORE

58

A True Caesar Salad

Yes, a true Caesar Salad is Mexican. It was invented at Caesar's Restaurant in Tijuana in 1929 and is not coated with thick dressing from a bottle. A proper Caesar Salad is assembled at the table and is dressed in the bowl. For your fiesta, however, you may wish to assemble it in the kitchen.

4 anchovy fillets, chopped small, divided

1 tsp Worcestershire sauce

1 tbsp red wine vinegar

2 tbsps olive oil

1/2 tsp sugar

1 clove garlic, minced

1/4 tsp cayenne pepper

2 to 3 large heads romaine lettuce

about 2 cups garlic croutons

2 tbsps capers

2 eggs

1/2 cup grated Parmesan cheese

1/2 tsp paprika

salt and black pepper, to taste

sweet purple onion, thinly sliced (optional)

Put two anchovies, Worcestershire sauce, vinegar, oil, sugar, garlic, and cayenne into large salad bowl. Use pestle or back of wooden spoon to mash into paste. Tear crisp inside lettuce leaves into bite-size pieces. Add to bowl; toss gently to coat evenly with paste. Add croutons, remaining two anchovies, and capers; toss gently. Put eggs into boiling water 1 minute; plunge immediately into ice water to stop cooking process. Crack eggs into salad and toss lightly. Add cheese, paprika, salt, and pepper; toss. Add a few onion rings, if desired.

❀ SERVES 6 TO 8

Jicama Salad

1 large jicama, peeled and diced

1 sweet purple onion, diced

1 fresh pineapple, diced (2 to 3 cups)

2 papayas, seeded and diced

1/4 cup fresh cilantro, chopped

1/4 cup fresh mint leaves, chopped,
   plus sprigs for garnish

1 small fresh hot chile, seeded and cut
   into very thin rings, to taste

1 cup Tamarind juice
   (or use fresh orange juice with two fresh
   limes squeezed into it to make one cup
   not the same but it's still nice)

1/4 cup olive oil

salt and black pepper, to taste

crisp lettuce leaves

avocados, sliced

seedless oranges, sliced

Put all ingredients except avocado, oranges, and lettuce into bowl and marinate about 1 hour. When ready to serve, line serving platter with lettuce, pile marinated ingredients onto lettuce, and surround salad with avocado and orange slices. Add fresh mint sprigs, and you have a beautiful creation. Serve cold.

❀ SERVES 6 TO 8

Pepper and Corn Salad

2 each red, yellow, and green peppers,
    roasted (see directions, page 45),
    julienned

2 to 3 Anaheim chiles, roasted
    (see directions, page 45), cut into rings

2 jalapeño chiles, roasted (see directions,
    page 45), cut into thin rings, to taste

corn kernels from 4 or 5 ears fresh corn

2 to 3 stalks celery, diced

1 sweet purple onion, diced

3 or 4 green onions including green,
    chopped

1 6 ounce can black olives, pitted
    and drained

1/2 cup fresh cilantro, chopped

vinaigrette (see recipe to right)

black pepper

crisp lettuce

Gently toss all ingredients together in
bowl. Drizzle vinaigrette; toss lightly.
Add pepper to taste. Serve on bed of
lettuce.

Vinaigrette:

1/3 cup olive oil

6 to 8 cloves garlic, roasted
    (see directions, page 45)

1 anchovy fillet

1/2 tsp cumin seeds

1 tsp Mexican oregano or Italian
    seasoning

1/2 tsp salt

1 tsp sugar

2/3 cup red wine vinegar

Tabasco-style hot sauce, to taste

Put oil, garlic, anchovy, cumin seeds,
oregano, salt, and sugar into mortar
and pestle or blender; blend into
paste. Add vinegar and mix thoroughly, adding tobasco to taste. For thinner
vinaigrette add a bit more vinegar and
oil. Taste and adjust seasonings as
needed.

❀ SERVES 8 TO 10

Chayote and Tomato Salad

3 to 4 chayote*
3 or 4 tomatoes
2 stalks celery
2 green onions including green, chopped
1 sweet purple onion, cut into thin rings
1/4 cup fresh cilantro, chopped
1/4 cup fresh mint leaves, minced
1 tbsp fresh oregano, minced
salt and black pepper, to taste
vinaigrette (see recipe to right)
crisp lettuce

Cut each chayote in half lengthwise (do not remove the edible seed), then cut across into slices about 1/8-inch thick. Blanch chayote lightly, chill, and drain. Cut tomatoes into wedges. Cut celery into 1-inch lengths, then julienne. Add remaining ingredients and toss lightly. Drizzle vinaigrette over salad and serve on bed of crisp letuce.

* a firm-fleshed, mild-flavored squash

Vinaigrette:

1/4 cup cider vinegar
1/4 cup lime juice
1/4 cup olive oil
1 tsp Worcestershire sauce
1 tbsp sugar, to taste
1 tsp chile powder, to taste

Put all ingredients into bowl and whisk vigorously.

❁ SERVES 6 TO 8

Zesty Bean Salad

about 1 cup each: garbanzo beans, pinto beans, red beans, and black beans, canned or from scratch (see directions for cooking beans, page 99), rinsed and drained

2 cups green beans, cut into 2-inch lengths, lightly blanched

1 sweet purple onion, chopped

2 to 3 green onions, chopped

2 stalks celery, chopped

1 sweet red bell pepper, seeded and cut into thin julienne

2 canned chipotle chiles, chopped, to taste

1/2 cup fresh cilantro, chopped

dressing (see recipe to right)

crisp lettuce leaves

tomato slices, for garnish

cucumber slices, for garnish

Put all ingredients into large bowl, add dressing, and toss gently. Line serving bowl with lettuce; pile salad into center. Garnish with fresh tomato and cucumber slices. This salad is sometimes served with alternate slices of cold beef and tomatoes around edge of serving plate.

Dressing:

1/2 cup cider vinegar

1/4 cup olive oil

juice of 2 limes

5 to 6 cloves garlic, chopped

2 tbsps tomato paste

2 fresh tomatoes, chopped

1 tbsp sugar, to taste

salt and black pepper, to taste

Put all ingredients into blender and process until smooth. Or, make a simple and delicious dressing by mixing equal amounts of mayonnaise and salsa of choice.

✿ SERVES 10 TO 12

Fiesta Cut-Up Potato Salad

6 to 8 large potatoes

2 sweet purple onions, diced

6 to 8 cloves garlic, minced

pickled jalapeño chiles, seeded and
very finely chopped, to taste

2 each red and green bell peppers,
seeded and diced

2 to 3 stalks celery, diced

1 cup Napoles, diced (jarred, prepared
cactus pads often available in
Mexican markets)

about 2 cups fresh or frozen corn kernels

2 to 3 cups cooked chicken, diced

4 hard-boiled eggs, diced, plus additional
sliced for garnish

1/2 cup fresh cilantro, chopped

1 cup mayonnaise

1 cup salsa of choice
(commercial or see recipes, pages
37–41)

salt and black pepper, to taste

crisp lettuce leaves

tomato slices

avocado slices

Drain, peel, and cool potatoes. Cut into bite-size pieces and put into large bowl. Add onions, garlic, chiles, peppers, celery, Napoles, corn, chicken, diced eggs, and cilantro; toss lightly. Combine mayonnaise and salsa, mix well, and add enough to moisten salad. Season with salt and pepper. Line large serving platter with lettuce; pile salad into center. Surround with tomato, avocado, and hard-boiled egg slices for festive garnish.

❀ SERVES 10 TO 12

Seafood-Stuffed Avocados and Tomatoes

6 large ripe avocados, 12 large ripe tomatoes,
  or a combination

fresh lime juice

3 cups cooked baby shrimp, crabmeat, imitation crab,
  or a combination

2 stalks celery, diced small

2 green onions including most of green part,
  chopped small

1 sweet purple onion, diced small

about 2 cups iceberg lettuce, finely shredded

1/2 cup fresh cilantro, finely chopped

1/2 cup chunky salsa of choice, drained
  (commercial or see recipes, pages 37–41)

1 cup mayonnaise

1/4 cup cocktail sauce

salt and black pepper, to taste

lettuce leaves

fresh lime wedges

Cut avocados in half, remove seeds, and peel. Sprinkle with lime juice to prevent browning. Set aside. Cut tops off tomatoes; remove pulp with tablespoon and discard or save for another use. Set upside down to drain. Mix seafood, celery, onions, lettuce, and cilantro together. Mix salsa, mayonnaise, and cocktail sauce together well; add enough to seafood mixture to moisten well. Season with salt and pepper. Spoon into avocados and tomatoes. Line serving plate with lettuce. Arrange avocados and tomatoes on plate and garnish with lime wedges.

✤ MAKES 12

Sure to Please Taco Salad

Taco salads are traditionally served in deep-fried flour tortilla shells, difficult to do if you are serving one large salad buffet style. The solution: a big bowl of salad and a pile of deep-fried taco shells to hold the salad.

1 or 2 sweet purple onions, diced

3 or 4 green onions including most of green part, chopped small

2 or 3 stalks celery, diced small

1 each red and green bell pepper, seeded and diced

1 can red beans, drained and rinsed

2 or 3 pickled jalapeño chiles, sliced into thin rings, to taste

about 1 cup pitted black olives, sliced

2 tbsps capers

1 small head iceberg lettuce, shredded

inner leaves of 1 head romaine lettuce, torn into small pieces

1 pound lean ground beef, sautéed or 3 cups chicken, cooked

dressing (see recipe to right)

salt and black pepper, to taste

4 hard-boiled eggs, sliced

deep-fried flour tortilla shells

Dressing:

1 cup mayonnaise

1 cup salsa of choice

1/2 cup ketchup

1 tbsp taco seasoning

Tabasco-style hot sauce, to taste

Mix all ingredients together well.

Put onions, celery, peppers, beans, chiles, olives, capers, and lettuce into large bowl; toss gently. Drain beef or dice chicken; add and toss. Add enough dressing to adequately moisten; toss gently. Transfer to large salad bowl; scatter eggs over salad. Serve with tortilla shells. You can fry them yourself or purchase them already fried.

❄ SERVES AT LEAST 10 TO 12

Tropical Fruit Fiesta

1 large ripe pineapple

5 or 6 large seedless oranges

1 sweet purple onion

3 or 4 ripe avocados

2 or 3 papayas

5 or 6 kiwi

fresh lime juice

turbinado or raw sugar

cinnamon

fresh lime wedges, for garnish

fresh mint sprigs, for garnish

Cut top off pineapple and reserve. Remove skin and core; cut into thin spears. Peel oranges; slice into thin rings. Peel onion; slice into thin rings. Cut avocados in half, remove pits, and cut into slices. Cut papayas in half, remove seeds, peel, and cut into slices. Peel and slice kiwi. Set pineapple top in center of large, attractive serving platter. Arrange fruit around top in attractive pattern. Sprinkle liberally with lime juice; sprinkle sparingly with sugar and cinnamon. Garnish with lime wedges and mint sprigs.

❀ SERVES AT LEAST 8 TO 10

Platillos de la Cena

Main Dishes

A Tortilla Manifesto

Tortillas are an integral part of Mexican cuisine. Not only are they used in the form we gringos have become familiar with — to make burritos, tacos, tostada, etc. — but also they are used to accompany food in the same way we accompany a meal with bread.

No recipe is included for making tortillas because they are a study in tedium and frustration. I am an experienced cook and also very detail and craft oriented, but in forty years I have yet to master tortillas. Store-bought varieties are often just as good; I strongly recommend using them.

Do-it-Yourself Burrito Buffet

Burritos ("small burros") are not an original part of Mexican cuisine. The use of "burritos" in relation to food didn't appear until after the 1930s. Burritos are a product of southwestern U.S. culture, and flour tortillas are far more popular in the States than in Mexico.

A burrito buffet is one of the most festive, fun, and easy ways to entertain, especially for a crowd. Prepare the following foods, which go well in burritos. Slice or chop, put into bowls or arrange on plates, garnish, display attractively on your table, and let guests assemble their own.

Tortillas:

Buy flour tortillas in desired size, wrap in aluminum foil, and heat in a 350-degree oven for about 10 minutes, or until they are the desired temperature. Or, wrap in a moist tea towel and microwave for about 2 minutes. Just before serving and place in a basket lined with clean cloths or in a covered stoneware dish. You can reheat in the microwave using the same moistened cloth.

Meats:

Use cooked meat like beef, pork, or chicken, or lightly sauté ground meats like chorizo (Mexican sausage). Supermarket-roasted chickens work well: pull off the skin and shred the meat. You can make already cooked meats more flavorful by adding sauce or salsa. Put in a resealable plastic bag, massage to distribute flavors, and leave in refrigerator until ready to serve. Reheat if desired by placing in a covered dish and heat in a 350-degree oven until desired temperature. You may also reheat in a microwave.

Vegetable Fillings:

refried beans, canned or from scratch
  (see Bean Tutorial, page 99)

Rancheros Rice (see recipe, page 103)

cheese, grated

green and yellow onions, diced

sweet red bell peppers, diced

hot chiles and pickled jalapeños, chopped

black olives, chopped

fresh cilantro and mint leaves, chopped

tomatoes, chopped

avocados, diced

crisp lettuce, shredded

guacamole (see recipes, page 24)

salsas (see recipes, pages 37–41)

sour cream

Breakfast Enchiladas

filling (see recipe to right)

about 3 cups Rojo Chile Sauce, commercial (enchilada sauce)
   or from scratch (see recipe, page 43)

olive oil or lard

12 to 15 corn tortillas

queso fresco or ricotta

fresh cilantro, chopped, plus sprigs for garnish

mozzarella cheese or Mexican equivalent, grated

lime wedges

Preheat oven to 350 degrees. Put about half of sauce in shallow dish or pan. Heat 1/2-inch layer oil in heavy skillet over moderate heat. Put one tortilla at a time in oil using tongs. Allow to soften without frying (30–60 seconds). Remove from oil, dip both sides in sauce, and transfer to flat plate. Place 2–3 tablespoons filling along one end of tortilla. Sprinkle with queso fresco and chopped cilantro; roll gently but firmly. Place in baking dish seam side down.

Continue until all tor tillas are filled, top with remaining sauce, and sprinkle with mozzarella cheese. Cover lightly with aluminum foil and bake 15–20 minutes. Remove foil and continue baking until cheese is melted and just beginning to brown. Garnish with fresh cilantro sprigs and serve with fresh lime wedges.

✿ MAKES 12 TO 15

Filling:

1/2 pound chorizo
   (Mexican sausage)

1/2 pound bulk sausage

8 eggs, beaten

salt, to taste

black pepper, to taste

fat from sausages, olive oil,
   or lard

1 large yellow onion, chopped

6 to 8 cloves garlic, minced

1 large red bell pepper,
   chopped

2 Anaheim chiles, chopped

about one cup of corn kernels,
   fresh or canned

Gently sauté chorizo and sausage in heavy skillet. Remove with slotted spoon and set aside. Beat eggs and season with salt and pepper. Using fat from sausage and chorizo, olive oil, or lard, gently scramble eggs. Remove from pan and set aside. Add more oil to pan if necessary; lightly sauté onions, garlic, pepper, and chiles until soft and just beginning to brown around the edges. Add corn and sauté 1 minute. Remove and set aside.

Beef Enchiladas in Salsa Rojo

2 to 3 tbsps olive oil

2 yellow onions, diced

8 to 10 cloves garlic, minced

1 Anaheim chile, seeded and chopped

1 small hot chile, seeded and minced, to taste

3 to 4 cups shredded beef
1/4 cup fresh cilantro, chopped

about 2 cups Rojo Chile Sauce, commercial (enchilada sauce) or from scratch (see recipe, page 43)

about 1 cup beef stock, canned or from scratch (see Stock Tutorial, page 47)

12 large corn tortillas

1/2 cup cheddar, grated

1/2 cup mozzarella, grated

Preheat oven to 350 degrees. Heat oil in heavy skillet over moderate heat and lightly sauté onions and garlic. Add chiles and sauté until soft and hot but not beginning to brown. Allow to cool; put into bowl with beef and cilantro. Pour sauce and stock into skillet, mix thoroughly, and heat. Dip tortillas into sauce mixture one at a time and lay on plate or other flat surface. Put 2–3 tablespoons of beef mixture in one end of tortilla, carefully roll up, and put into baking dish with seam side down. Continue until all tortillas are filled, top with remaining sauce mixture. Cover with foil and bake 35–45 minutes or until sauce is bubbling and enchiladas are beginning to brown around the edges. Mix cheeses together and sprinkle over enchiladas. Return to oven and bake until cheeses are melted. Serve hot. (NOTE: Enchiladas can be assembled in advance and frozen until ready to cook.)

✸ SERVES 4 TO 6

Bean and Cheese Enchiladas

3 to 4 cups refried beans, canned or
  from scratch (see recipe, page 99)

1 yellow onion, chopped

1/4 cup fresh cilantro,
  chopped

1/2 cup sharp cheddar cheese,
  grated

1/2 cup mozzarella cheese, grated

2 cups Rojo Chile Sauce, commercial (enchilada sauce)
  or from scratch (see recipe, page 43)

1 cup queso fresco or ricotta cheese

12 large corn tortillas

Preheat oven to 350 degrees. Mix beans with onion and cilantro; set aside. Toss together cheddar cheese and mozzarella cheese; reserve 1/3 cup for later use. Heat sauce in skillet over moderate heat and dip in 1 tortilla long enough to soften slightly. Transfer tortilla to plate and gently spread one side with about 2 tablespoons of bean mixture. Sprinkle some quesa fresca over top with a bit of grated cheese mixture. Roll up, place into baking dish seam side down, and repeat until all tortillas are filled.

Pour remaining sauce over enchiladas, cover and bake 30 to 40 minutes or until sauce is bubbling and edges of enchiladas are beginning to brown. Remove cover and sprinkle top with reserved cheese mixture. Return to oven until cheese melts. (NOTE: Enchiladas can be assembled in advance and frozen until ready to cook.)

❀ SERVES 4 TO 6

Ground Meat and Vegetable Enchiladas

filling (see recipe at right)

Rojo Chile Sauce, commercial or from scratch (see recipe, page 43)

olive oil or lard

12 to 15 corn tortillas

shredded lettuce

green onion, finely chopped, including greens

queso fresco or feta, crumbled

fresh cilantro, chopped

pickled jalapeños, chopped

NOTE: Enchiladas can be assembled in advance and frozen until ready to cook.

Preheat oven to 350 degrees. Heat 1/2-inch layer oil in heavy skillet over moderate heat and fry tortillas (one at a time) until softened but not browned. Dip tortilla in sauce and lay on flat surface or plate. Put 2–3 tablespoons filling across tortilla, roll gently but firmly, and place seam side down in baking dish. Continue until all tortillas are filled; pour remaining sauce over top. Cover dish with foil, and bake 20–30 minutes. Serve with garnish buffet of lettuce, onion, queso fresco, cilantro, and jalapeños.

Filling:

1/2 pound ground beef

1/2 pound ground pork

2 to 3 tbsps olive oil or lard

1 large onion, chopped

8 to 10 cloves garlic, minced

1 stalk celery, chopped

1 large bell pepper, seeded and chopped

2 Anaheim chiles, seeded and chopped

2 medium potatoes, peeled and diced

1 medium zucchini, chopped

3 or 4 tomatoes, chopped

2 tsps Mexican oregano or favorite herbs

1/2 tsp cumin seeds

about 1 cup beef stock, canned or from scratch (see Stock Tutorial, page 47)

about 1/2 cup corn kernels fresh, frozen or canned

1/2 cup fresh cilantro, chopped

salt, to taste

black pepper, to taste

Lightly sauté meat in heavy skillet. Drain fat, remove meat from skillet, and set aside. Wipe skillet clean, heat oil over moderate heat, and gently sauté onion and garlic until soft, translucent, and beginning to brown. Add celery, pepper, chiles, potatoes, and zucchini; continue to sauté until beginning to soften. Add tomatoes, oregano, and cumin seeds and sauté 2–3 minutes. Add meat and stock and simmer until vegetables are soft and most liquid is absorbed. Chop corn and cilantro and add to skillet. Season with salt and pepper and cook 2–3 minutes.

❀ SERVES 6 TO 8

Grilled Chicken Fajitas

2 to 3 tbsps olive oil

1 small onion, cut into thin rings

3 to 4 cloves garlic, very thinly sliced

1 red bell pepper, seeded and sliced thin

4 boneless chicken breasts, skinned
    and cut into thin strips

1 tsp paprika

1/4 tsp ground cumin

1/4 tsp dry chile flakes, to taste

1/4 tsp dried oregano

about 1/2 cup chicken stock, canned or
    from scratch (see Stock Tutorial, page 47)

1/2 cup fresh cilantro, chopped

1 lime, juiced

1 tomato, chopped plus 1 tomato, sliced

1 avocado, peeled and chopped plus 1
    avocado, peeled and sliced

salt, to taste

black pepper, to taste

12 warm flour tortillas (see Tortillas in
    Do-It-Yourself Burrito Buffet, page 73)

salsa, commercial or from scratch
    (see recipes, pages 37–41)

Heat oil in heavy skillet to moderate and gently sauté onion, garlic, and pepper until soft. Add chicken and continue to sauté until chicken reaches desired doneness. Add paprika, cumin, chile flakes, oregano, and stock; sauté a few more minutes. Remove from heat, add cilantro, lime juice, chopped tomato, and chopped avocado. Toss gently and season with salt and pepper. Put on serving platter; garnish with avocado slices, tomato slices, and cilantro sprigs. Accompany with tortillas and salsa.

✿ SERVES 4 TO 6

Steak & Pepper Fajitas

1/4 cup olive oil, plus additional for frying

1/2 cup red wine vinegar

5 1/3 tablespoons sugar, divided

3 tbsps chile seasoning, divided

3 limes, juiced and divided

1 tsp oregano

1/2 tsp cumin seeds, crushed

8 cloves garlic, finely minced and divided

salt, to taste, divided

black pepper, to taste, divided

1 to 1 1/2 pounds lean boneless steak

2 onions, cut into thin rings

1/2 each red, green, and yellow bell pepper, seeded and sliced thin

about 1/4 cup beef broth, canned or from scratch (see Stock Tutorial, page 47)

dry chile flakes, to taste

1/2 cup fresh cilantro, chopped, plus sprigs for garnish

1 to 2 lemons, wedged (optional)

12 warm flour tortillas (see Tortillas in Do-It-Yourself Burrito Buffet, page 73)

salsa, commercial or from scratch (see recipes, pages 37–41)

Put oil, vinegar, 4 tablespoons sugar, 2 tablespoons chile seasoning, juice from two limes, oregano, cumin seeds, and four garlic cloves in large resealable plastic bag. Mix well. Season with salt and pepper; add steak. Seal bag and massage to work marinade into meat. Marinate 1 hour. Grill or broil steak to desired doneness and let sit 5 minutes before slicing; set aside.

Heat oil in heavy skillet to moderate. Gently sauté onions and remaining four garlic cloves until onions are soft and beginning to turn golden around edges. Add peppers and continue to sauté until mostly soft. Add broth, remaining 1 1/3 tablespoons sugar, remaining 1 tablespoon chile seasoning, remaining juice from one lime, and chile flakes; toss gently to distribute evenly. Season with salt and pepper. Cook gently 2–3 minutes, add 1/2 cup cilantro, toss carefully, and remove from heat. Arrange steak and pepper-onion mixture on serving platter; garnish with lemon wedges and cilantro sprigs. Accompany with tortillas and salsa.

❀ SERVES 4 TO 6

Garden Fajitas

1/4 cup olive oil, plus additional for frying

1/2 cup red wine vinegar

1/4 cup sugar

2 tbsps tomato paste

2 limes, juiced plus 1 to 2 limes, wedged
(optional)

2 tbsps chile seasoning

1 tsp oregano

1/2 tsp cumin seeds, crushed

dry crushed chile flakes, to taste

6 to 8 cloves garlic, very finely minced

salt, to taste, divided

black pepper, to taste, divided

1 pound firm tofu, cut into 1/2-inch cubes

1 large yellow onion, thinly sliced with
rings cut in half

2 small zucchini, cut into 3-inch slices

2 sweet red peppers, seeded and sliced

1/4 cup fresh cilantro, chopped, plus
sprigs for garnish

12 warm flour tortillas (see Tortillas in
Do-It-Yourself Burrito Buffet, page 73)

salsa, commercial or from scratch
(see recipes, pages 37–41)

Put oil, vinegar, sugar, tomato paste, lime juice, chile seasoning, oregano, cumin seeds, chile flakes, garlic, salt, and pepper in large resealable plastic bag and massage thoroughly to totally integrate ingredients. Add tofu, onion, zucchini, and peppers; marinate at least 1 hour or refrigerate overnight. Heat oil in heavy skillet to moderate and gently sauté contents of bag until mostly soft and hot throughout, being careful not to break up tofu. Season with salt and pepper, add cilantro, and remove from heat. Arrange tofu mixture on serving platter and garnish with lime wedges, if using, and cilantro sprigs. Accompany with tortillas and salsa.

❀ SERVES 4 TO 6

Vegetable Pie

olive oil

2 large yellow onions, I chopped, I cut
　　into thin rings and separated

8 to10 cloves garlic, chopped small

I serrano chile, seeded and cut into
　　very thin rings

3 cups cooked Salsa Verde
　　(commercial or see recipe, page 41)

I cup prepared bouillon or vegetable stock
　　(commercial or see recipe, page 47)

salt and black pepper, to taste

about 3 cups refried beans, divided
　　(canned or see recipe, page 99)

corn cut from about 3 ears corn, or
　　about 2 cups frozen

2 ripe red peppers, roasted and cut
　　into rings (see recipe, page 45)

3 to 4 small zucchini, sliced into thin rings

15 to 20 tortillas, depending on size

grated cheese, for garnish

sour cream, for garnish

Heat 2–3 tablespoons oil in heavy skillet and gently sauté chopped onion, garlic, and chile until soft and just beginning to brown. Add salsa and stock and bring to boil. Reduce heat and continue to simmer 35–45 minutes or until thickened and somewhat reduced.

Add salt and pepper. Heat oil in another heavy skillet and lightly sauté onion rings until soft, translucent, and just beginning to brown; set onions aside and wipe out pan.

Preheat oven to 350 degrees. Heat about 1/4 inch oil in the heavy skillet, heat several tortillas to soften, and dip in sauce. Line 9 x 14-inch baking pan or Mexican pottery equivalent with softened tortillas. Spread about 1 cup beans over tortillas. Sprinkle some corn over beans, then lay some onion rings over corn. Scatter some peppers and zucchini on top. Spoon some sauce over all. Continue until pan is full. Top with sauce and bake 35–45 minutes or until bubbling and beginning to brown. Remove from oven and let sit 10 minutes before serving. Accompany with bowls of grated cheese and sour cream for garnish.

❋ SERVES AT LEAST 8 TO 10

Mushroom and Tortilla Casserole

In Mexico this dish is often made with cuiclacoche, a much-prized fungus that grows on corn. Because this delicacy is virtually unheard of north of the border, mushrooms may be substituted.

3 to 4 tbsps olive oil, plus additional for frying

2 to 3 yellow onions, sliced into thin rings and separated

8 to 10 cloves garlic, chopped small

2 to 3 serrano chiles, seeded and chopped small, to taste

about 2 1/2 pounds mushrooms including stems, sliced

about 3 cups cooked Salsa Rojo (commercial chile sauce or see recipe, page 43), divided (any red sauce, chili sauce, or salsa can be used)

1 cup chicken or vegetarian stock, broth, or bouillon (commercial or see recipe, page 47)

1/2 cup fresh cilantro, chopped

salt and black pepper, to taste

12 to 15 corn tortillas, depending on size

about 3 cups mozzarella cheese or Mexican equivalent, grated

Heat oil in heavy skillet and gently sauté onions, garlic, chiles, and mushrooms until soft, translucent, and just beginning to brown. (You may need a bit more oil because mushrooms are quite absorbent.) Add sauce and stock and bring to boil. Immediately reduce heat to maintain a simmer and cook about 15 to 20 minutes or until a mushroom sauce is formed. Add cilantro, salt, and pepper. If you like a spicier dish, add a few dry chile flakes or a bit of Tabasco-style hot sauce. Set aside.

Preheat oven to 350 degrees. Heat about 1/4 inch olive oil in heavy skillet and lightly fry several tortillas until hot through but not beginning to harden. Remove tortillas, using tongs, and drain on paper towels. Line 9 x 14-inch baking dish or Mexican pottery equivalent with drained tortillas. Pour 1 layer of mushroom mixture over tortilla layer and sprinkle with cheese. Top with more heated and drained tortillas, mushroom mixture, and cheese. Continue until pan is full, usually about three layers. Top with the remaining sauce and sprinkle with cheese. Bake until hot and bubbling, 25-30 minutes. Allow to cool about 10 minutes before serving.

❋ SERVES AT LEAST 8 TO 10

Grilled Prawns Piquante

2 to 2 1/2 pounds large prawns

1/2 cup lime juice

1/4 cup olive oil

1/4 cup sugar, to taste

1/2 tsp fresh ginger root, grated

1/2 tsp jalapeño chile, very finely minced

1/4 cup fresh cilantro, very finely minced

4 cloves garlic, very finely minced

1 tbsp chile powder

salt and black pepper, to taste

lime wedges

bamboo skewers

Peel, devein, and wash prawns, leaving tails on; pat dry. Place in large resealable plastic bag. Mix remaining ingredients together and place in bag with prawns. Massage gently; refrigerate several hours before grilling, kneading periodically.

Soak skewers in water about 20 minutes to prevent them from burning. Thread four prawns on each skewer. To prevent prawns from spinning around on the skewer, use two skewers side by side. I usually place 4 prawns per pair of skewers. Place skewers on prepared grill and cook to desired degree of doneness, turning once, 2–3 minutes on each side or until prawns are opaque. If you don't have a grill, you can cook them under the oven broiler. Paint several times with remaining marinade during grilling. Serve with lime wedges.

❀ SERVES 4 TO 6

Fiesta Mixed Seafood Grill

2 dried ancho or poblano chiles

boiling water

1/2 cup lime juice

1/4 cup olive oil

1/4 cup sugar, to taste

1/2 tsp fresh ginger root, grated

1/2 tsp jalapeño chile, very finely minced

1/4 cup fresh cilantro, very finely minced

4 to 6 cloves garlic, very finely minced

1 tbsp chile powder

1 tsp dry dill weed

salt and black pepper, to taste

1 pound large prawns, peeled and
    deveined, leaving tails on

1 pound salmon, cut into 1-inch cubes

1 pound firm-flesh white fish, cut into
    1-inch cubes

1 pound large scallops

lime wedges

bamboo skewers

Put dried chiles into bowl and pour boiling water over them. Let sit 20–30 minutes. When chiles are softened, remove stems and put chiles into blender with just enough soaking water to process; puree. Strain; put into bowl. Add all remaining ingredients except seafood. Mix well, taste, and adjust seasonings. Put in large resealable plastic bag, add seafood, and refrigerate about 1 hour.

Soak skewers in water about 30 minutes. When ready to grill, thread seafood onto skewers. Place on grill and cook to desired degree of doneness, turning once or twice. Seafood should be opaque. Time will vary depending on type of fish used. Serve with lime wedges for squeezing over skewers. This is particularly good served with green rice and Caesar salad.

❀ SERVES 6 TO 8

85

BBQ'd Orange Chicken

2 to 3 dried ancho or poblano chiles

boiling water

2 large chickens, cut into serving pieces

1 tbsp salt, plus additional to taste

1 tbsp black pepper, plus additional to taste

2 tbsps sugar, plus additional if needed

2 tbsp chile powder, divided

juice of 2 to 3 limes

1/4 cup olive oil

1/4 cup frozen orange juice concentrate

1/2 cup orange marmalade

6 to 8 cloves garlic, finely minced

*1 small hot chile, seeded and
    very finely minced, to taste*

1/4 cup fresh cilantro, finely minced

fresh oregano sprigs, very finely minced

1/2 tsp cumin seeds

Remove stems and seeds from dried chiles; put chiles in bowl and cover with boiling water. Let sit 15–20 minutes. Cut chicken into serving pieces, rinse under cold running water, pat dry, and place on dish. Mix together 1 tablespoon salt, 1 tablespoon pepper, sugar, and 1 tablespoon chile powder. Rub mixture onto chicken pieces; be sure to rub onto all surfaces.

Sprinkle lime juice over chicken and set aside.

Put soaked chiles into blender with enough soaking water to process; puree. Strain; scrape into bowl with remaining ingredients and mix well. Season with salt and pepper to taste and additional sugar if needed. For spicier chicken, add a few dry chile flakes. Paint chicken while broiling, grilling, or barbequing to desired degree of doneness. To test for doneness, cut into thickest part of the chicken. Meat should be opaque, not translucent. Thick slices of onion painted with sauce and broiled or grilled are a nice addition.

❀ SERVES 8 TO 10

Grilled Chicken in Salsa Verde

2 chickens cut into serving pieces

2 cups Salsa Verde (see recipe, page 41), plus additional
*   for grilling (optional)*

olive oil

fresh cilantro, minced for garnish

freshly squeezed lime juice, for garnish

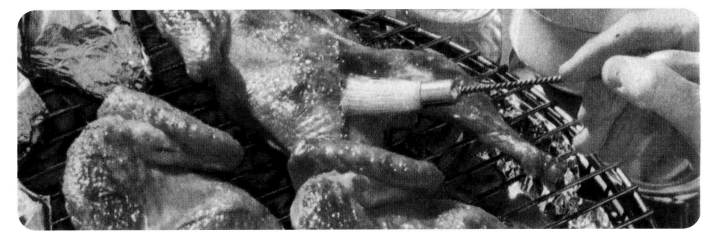

Wash chicken and pat dry. Put in large resealable plastic bag with Salsa Verde
and oil to cover. Seal and massage salsa into chicken. Refrigerate several hours
or until ready to grill, massaging every hour. Shake off excess salsa and place
chicken, skin side down, on hot grill. Paint chicken with extra Salsa Verde two
or three times during grilling, if desired. Cook, turning once, until chicken is
done. To test for doneness, cut into thickest part of one piece using small sharp
knife. Meat should appear opaque. Pile chicken on serving platter; sprinkle with
cilantro and lime juice.

❋ SERVES 6 TO 8

Pineapple and Pork

2 to 3 tbsps olive oil

2 to 2 1/2 pounds lean pork, cut into
  1-inch cubes

2 yellow onions, chopped

4 cloves garlic, minced

1 jalapeño chile, seeded and cut into
  very thin rings, to taste

about 2 cups fresh or canned
  pineapple chunks

1 cup defatted chicken stock, broth,
  or bouillon

1 cup pineapple juice

2 tbsps sugar

1/4 cup fresh cilantro, chopped

1/4 cup fresh mint, chopped

juice of 2 limes

salt and black pepper, to taste

Heat oil in heavy skillet; sear pork on all sides. Add onions, garlic, and chile; sauté until soft but not yet browned. Add pineapple chunks; toss together. Add stock, pineapple juice, and sugar. Stir, reduce heat to simmer, cover, and cook until pork is tender. Remove cover and reduce liquid until thick sauce forms. Add cilantro, mint, and lime juice. Season with salt and pepper; simmer a few minutes. Serve with rice.

❀ SERVES 4 TO 6

Party Time Piggy in a Pot

2 to 3 tbsps olive oil

1 3 1/2- to 4-pound pork roast (shoulder is a good choice)

1 large onion, diced, plus 1 or 2 yellow onions cut into thick slices

8 to 10 cloves garlic, chopped, plus 15 to 20 whole cloves, peeled

1 jalapeño chile, seeded and cut into thin rings, to taste

1 large bell pepper, seeded and diced

2 tbsps chile powder

2 tbsps sugar

1 tsp cumin seeds, crushed

1 tsp cinnamon

1 tsp ground ginger

2 to 3 cups beef stock, broth, or bouillon (commercial or see recipe, page 47)

1 bay leaf

about 1 pound small boiling onions, peeled

about 1 pound smallest new potatoes, unpeeled

3 to 4 Anaheim chiles

2 to 3 red bell peppers, seeded and quartered

salt and black pepper, to taste

1/2 cup cilantro, chopped

warm corn tortillas

Preheat oven to 325 degrees. In large heavy skillet, heat oil and brown pork well on all sides. Remove and set aside. Add a bit more oil if necessary to skillet and gently sauté diced onion, chopped garlic, jalapeño, and diced pepper until just beginning to brown. Add seasonings, stir well, and cook over moderate heat, stirring, about 1 minute. Remove from heat.

To keep meat from sticking and possibly scorching, place sliced onions on bottom of heavy ovenproof baking dish with tight-fitting lid. Set meat on onions. Surround with vegetables and seasonings. Add peeled garlic cloves, bouillon, and bay leaf. Cover and bake about 2 1/2-3 hours or until meat is extremely tender. Add a bit more stock from time to time if meat looks like it may become dry. When meat is fork tender, add boiling onions, potatoes, chiles, and peppers. Cover, raise heat to 350 degrees, and cook about 30 minutes or until vegetables are tender. Remove from oven and let cool about 15 minutes. Arrange meat and vegetables on serving platter. Skim as much fat as possible from liquid and season with salt and pepper; stir in cilantro. Slice meat; pour pan juices over all. Serve with tortillas.

❀ SERVES 6 TO 8

Chicken in Orange and Ancho Glaze

2 large chickens, split in half

6 tbsps sugar, divided

1 tbsp chile powder

1 tsp salt, plus additional to taste

1 tsp black pepper, plus additional to taste

4 dry ancho chiles

boiling water

1 cup orange juice

1 tbsp orange zest

1 cup orange marmalade

6 cloves garlic, minced

1 small yellow onion, minced

2 small fresh hot chiles, seeded and finely minced, to taste

1/4 cup inexpensive cream Sherry

1/4 cup fresh cilantro, chopped, plus sprigs for garnish

orange slices, for garnish

Wash chickens inside and out; pat dry. Mix together 2 tablespoons sugar, chile powder, 1 teaspoon salt, and 1 teaspoon pepper; rub over chicken, covering all surfaces. Place on plate, cover, and let sit several hours or refrigerate overnight.

Open dry chiles and brush out seeds. Put chiles in bowl and cover with boiling water. Let sit about 30 minutes. When chiles are soft, put into blender or food processor with remaining ingredients and process, forming paste. Use some soaking liquid to process if necessary.

Strain to remove any bits. Put into small saucepan and simmer, stirring constantly, until sauce becomes somewhat translucent. Remove from heat and cool.

Paint all sides of chicken with sauce. If baking or broiling, place on wire rack over baking pan or broiler. Bake in 350-degree oven, or broil, to desired degree of doneness. to test for doneness cut into thickest part of the chicken. Meat should be opaque, not traslucent. If grilling, grill over moderate heat to desired degree of doneness. Paint with sauce several times during cooking. Garnish with cilantro sprigs and orange slices.

✿ SERVES 6 TO 8

Chicken Mole

Mole can be an arduous and time-consuming creation. Here is a lazy gringo version. No, it's not authentic, but it is tasty and it didn't take a week and the aid of all the saints to make. Although here the mole is served with chicken, it is also traditionally served with roast pork and turkey.

2 to 3 tbsps chile powder

1 to 2 tbsps sugar

1 tsp black pepper

1 tsp cinnamon

2 chickens cut into serving pieces

olive oil for frying

mole sauce (see recipe to right)

Mix chile powder, sugar, pepper, and cinnamon together well. Rinse chicken under cold running water and pat dry. Rub seasoning mixture onto chicken. Heat about 1/4 inch oil in heavy skillet and brown chicken well on all sides. Add to mole sauce, cover, and continue to simmer until chicken is tender. Remove to serving platter and garnish with sprinkling of minced cilantro and sesame seeds.

❀ SERVES 6 TO 8

Mole Sauce

3 to 4 dried ancho or poblano chiles

1/2 cup each almonds, peanuts, pine nuts, pumpkin seeds, and sesame seeds

1/4 cup olive oil or melted lard

1 onion, diced

6 to 8 cloves garlic, chopped

4 to 6 plum tomatoes, chopped

2 tbsps tomato paste

1 tbsp oregano, preferably Mexican

1/4 tsp cloves, powdered

1 tbsp cinnamon

1 tsp ground ginger

1/4 cup unsweetened cocoa

2 cups chicken stock, broth, or bouillon (commercial or see recipe, page 47)

1/4 cup sugar

dry chile flakes, to taste

salt and black pepper, to taste

Remove stems and seeds from chiles and put chiles in bowl. Cover with boiling water and let sit 20-30 minutes or until soft. Process in blender using soaking liquid to form thin paste. Gently toast each kind of seed and nut separately in heavy dry skillet. Grind together in blender or food processor into paste. Set aside. Heat oil in heavy skillet with tight-fitting lid and gently sauté onion and garlic until lightly browned. Add tomatoes and tomato paste and continue to sauté 1–2 minutes. Add oregano, cloves, cinnamon, ginger, cocoa, chile paste, and nut paste. Stir well; add stock, sugar, and chile flakes. Simmer 20–30 minutes or until slightly thickened and almost translucent. Taste and adjust seasonings. Season with salt and pepper. You may want a bit more sugar, cocoa, cinnamon, or chile flakes. If you add more heat, remember that although this dish does sport the subtle flavor of ancho or poblano chiles, it is not supposed to be a blow-the-top-of-your-head-off dish.

Roast Turkey with Cornbread/Chorizo Stuffing and Chipotle Glaze

your favorite cornbread recipe

about 1/2 pound chorizo sausage

about 1/2 pound bulk sausage

2 large yellow onions, diced

6 to 8 cloves garlic, chopped small

1/2 each green, red, and yellow bell
pepper, seeded and diced

1 or 2 canned chipotle chiles, minced,
to taste

2 stalks celery, chopped small

olive oil, if needed

1 tbsp chile powder, to taste

1 tbsp taco seasoning, to taste

1 tbsp Italian seasoning

1 tbsp sugar, to taste

salt and black pepper, to taste

turkey or chicken stock, broth, or bouillon
(commercial or see recipe, page 47)

1/2 cup cilantro, chopped

1 cup almonds, blanched and slivered

2 eggs, lightly beaten

1 turkey

Chipotle Glaze (see recipe on right)

Prepare cornbread and let cool or make the previous day. Crumble cornbread and place in large bowl. In large heavy skillet lightly sauté sausages, breaking pieces apart. Do not brown. Remove with slotted spoon and add to cornbread. Gently sauté onions, garlic, peppers, chiles, and celery in sausage fat. Add a bit more oil if needed. Sauté vegetables until only lightly browned. Add to cornbread. Add all seasonings and just enough stock to lightly moisten so stuffing will hold together if squeezed but will fall apart if dropped back into bowl. Taste and adjust seasonings. Mix in cilantro and almonds. Add eggs and mix gently but thoroughly. When stuffing is completely cooled, pack lightly into turkey cavity. (I always put some under the flap of skin in the neck opening as well.) Truss turkey and set on rack in baking pan. Follow baking instructions for stuffed turkey.

❀ SERVES 6 TO 8

Chipotle Glaze

1 cup Oriental sweet chile sauce for chicken

4 to 5 cloves garlic, minced

1 or 2 canned chipotle chiles, chopped

1 tsp taco seasoning

1/2 tsp cumin, ground

1/2 tsp Mexican oregano

1 tbsp cocoa powder

1/2 cup chicken or turkey stock, broth,
or bouillon

Put all ingredient in blender and puree. Strain. Taste and adjust seasonings. During the last 45 minutes of cooking the turkey, paint liberally with glaze every 10–15 minutes. If skin browns too quickly, cover turkey with foil tent. Paint again before bringing turkey to table.

Fish Fillets in Salsa Verde

salt

pepper

2 firm-flesh white fish fillets per person

fresh lime juice

cooked Salsa Verde (commercial or see recipe, page 41)

fresh cilantro sprigs

lime wedges

Salt and pepper both sides of fillets. Place on baking sheet and squeeze juice over fillets. Broil until edges begin to curl and tops are opaque. Gently turn over fillets; broil until just beginning to brown. Paint liberally with Salsa Verde; return to oven to heat. Remove to serving platter; garnish with cilantro sprigs and lime wedges. Serve extra Salsa Verde in separate bowl.

❋ SERVES 2 FILLETS PER PERSON

94

Poached Fish Fillets in Ancho Mayonnaise

In my opinion this dish is better cold than hot.

chicken stock or bouillon (commercial or see recipe, page 47)

1/4 cup vinegar

6 cloves garlic, crushed

1 serrano chile, split in half

1 bay leaf

1 nice-sized firm-flesh white fish steak per person

Ancho Mayonnaise (see recipe, page 44)

Garnish:

fresh cilantro sprigs

lime wedges

capers

black pepper

Pour about 1 inch stock in large heavy skillet. Add vinegar, garlic, chile, and bay leaf. Bring to boil. Reduce heat to maintain slow simmer and cook about 5 minutes. Remove garlic, chile, and bay leaf. Gently slide fish into poaching liquid and continue to simmer until fish is done. To test for doneness, pierce thickest part with tip of small sharp knife. Flesh should be opaque. Remove fish and let drain. Place on serving platter, put generous dollop of mayonnaise on each piece, and garnish with cilantro sprig, lime wedge, scattering of capers, and grinding of black pepper.

❁ SERVES 1 FISH STEAK PER PERSON

Tamale Pie

2 quarts boiling water

about 3 cups yellow cornmeal

2 tbsps chile powder

salt, to taste

filling (see recipe to right)

about 1/2 cup each cheddar and
    mozzarella cheese, grated

Bring water to boil; gradually pick up some cornmeal, scatter it into water, and stir constantly using wire wisk. When cornmeal has been incorporated, stir in chile powder. Reduce heat to simmer and continue to cook, stirring with wooden spoon, until mixture thickens. Add salt. When cool, line 9 x 14-inch baking pan or Mexican pottery equivalent on bottom and sides with cornmeal, about 1/2-inch thick.

Preheat oven to 350 degrees. Pour filling into lined baking dish. Sprinkle with cheeses. Cover with aluminum foil and bake 50–60 minutes. Remove foil and bake uncovered until cheese melts and begins to brown. Cool 10–15 minutes before serving.

Filling:

1 1/2 pounds ground meat (beef, pork, or a combination), ground chicken, or ground turkey

1/2 pound chorizo (Mexican sausage)

olive oil

2 onions, diced

8 to 10 cloves garlic, minced

2 stalks celery, diced

1 red bell pepper, seeded and diced

2 Anaheim chiles, seeded and cut into very thin rings

3 to 4 tbsps tomato paste

4 to 6 large tomatoes, chopped

2 cups stock, broth or bouillon (commercial or see recipe, page 47)

2 to 3 tbsps chile powder

1/2 tsp cumin seeds

1 tsp oregano, preferably Mexican

1 tbsp Italian seasoning

1/4 cup sugar

1/4 cup red wine vinegar

dry chile flakes, to taste

1/2 cup fresh cilantro, chopped

salt and black pepper, to taste

To make filling:

Heat heavy skillet and lightly sauté meat and sausage, breaking pieces apart. Remove to plate using slotted spoon and reserve. Sauté onion, garlic, celery, pepper, and chiles. When soft, translucent, and just beginning to brown, add tomato paste, tomatoes, and stock. Stir well to incorporate tomato paste throughout; bring to boil. Reduce to simmer and add meat and sausage. Add chile powder, cumin seeds, oregano, Italian seasoning, sugar, vinegar, and chile flakes; simmer 45–60 minutes or until sauce is thick like rich spaghetti sauce. Stir in cilantro; season with salt and pepper.

❀ SERVES 8 TO 10

Variation: Vegetarian Tamale Pie

Substitute 2 cups cooked pinto beans and 2 cups fresh or frozen corn for meat and sausage; add with tomatoes. Use vegetarian stock (see recipe, page 47). Vegans can omit cheeses or use soy products.

Frijoles, Arroz, y Verduras
Beans, Rice, & Vegetables

Many side dishes can easily double as entrées, particularly if you are entertaining buffet style. Beans typically come to mind when I think of Mexican side dishes, but potatoes are New World, well adapted to Hispanic cuisines, and many folks enjoy eating them as much as they enjoy eating beans.

Refried Beans from a Can or from Scratch

3 to 4 tbsps olive oil or lard

2 white or yellow onions, diced

6 to 8 cloves garlic, minced

4 cups cooked beans, canned (2-oz. cans)
  or from scratch

chile powder, to taste

dry chile flakes, to taste

salt, to taste

black pepper, to taste

1/2 cup fresh cilantro, finely chopped

Heat oil in large heavy skillet and gently sauté onions and garlic until pinkish and translucent. Do not brown. Add cooked beans (drain if using canned) and begin frying over moderate heat. Mash beans with a vegetable masher as you fry them. Mashing can be as thorough as you wish, though leave some whole; I think they're better with some texture. Begin adding seasonings, and squash everything down in the skillet to allow browning to begin. Flip and mix beans slightly so the unbrowned layer is on the bottom of the pan. Continue until beans are hot and there are lovely, almost crisp bits scattered throughout. (You may have to add a bit more oil or lard as you cook.) Add cilantro, adjust seasonings, and use beans alone or in recipes.

✿ MAKES 5 TO 6 CUPS

BEAN TUTORIAL

The Basics of Beans:
To Soak or Not to Soak, That Is the Question

Soaking beans is an exercise in futility. I have never soaked a bean in my life (nor did my mother), and I have no idea where the myth about soaking and faster cooking came from. The theory that soaking beans removes gasses is also unfounded. Gaseous results have more to do with our not being used to high-fiber diets than with the beans themselves.

My method is simple: I put the beans in a pot that allows enough room for the beans and water, cover them with enough cold water so the water stands about 4 inches above the surface of the beans, bring them to a boil, and reduce the heat to maintain a simmer. Then I cover the pot with a tight-fitting lid, and in an hour and a half to an hour and forty-five minutes I have fully cooked beans! No soaking, no draining, no fussing!

Salt the beans after cooking because salting and then cooking tends to make them tough. You can, however, add garlic, onion, bay leaves, and other herbs and seasonings while the beans cook.

Two cups of dry beans will yield almost four cups of cooked beans

Fiesta Bean and Corn Skillet

2 to 3 tbsps olive oil or lard

1 large white or yellow onion, diced

6 to 8 cloves garlic, chopped

2 stalks celery, chopped small

1 large red bell pepper, seeded and diced

1 large green bell pepper, seeded
and diced

2 Anaheim chiles, seeded
and cut into thin rings

jalapeño peppers to taste, seeded and
cut into thin rings

6 cups cooked beans, canned
or from scratch
(see Bean Tutorial, page 99)

5 or 6 ears of corn or
1 16-oz. pkg frozen corn

1 cup beef, chicken, or vegetarian stock,
canned or from scratch (see Stock
Tutorial, page 47)

1 tbsp chile powder, to taste

1 tbsp sugar

salt, to taste

black pepper, to taste

2 to 3 tomatoes, cut into small wedges

3 to 4 green onions including most of
the green, cut into thin rings

1/2 cup fresh cilantro, chopped,
plus sprigs for garnish

1/4 cup fresh lime juice, to taste

lime wedges

Heat oil in large skillet and gently sauté onion and garlic until pinkish and translucent. Do not brown. Add celery, peppers, and chiles; continue to sauté until hot and somewhat wilted. Add beans, corn (cut from cobs if using fresh), stock, chile powder, salt, and pepper; continue to sauté over moderate heat, stirring occasionally to prevent scorching. Cook until most liquid has been absorbed. Add tomatoes, green onions, cilantro, and lime juice; cook only until mixture is hot. Put on serving platter and garnish with cilantro sprigs and lime wedges for a very colorful and festive presentation.

❀ SERVES AT LEAST 6 TO 8

Chorizo and Beans

1 pound chorizo (Mexican sausage)
olive oil or lard
2 white or yellow onions, diced
6 to 8 cloves garlic, minced
2 stalks celery, chopped
1 large red bell pepper, seeded
  and diced
1 large green bell pepper, seeded
  and diced
1 jalapeño pepper to taste, seeded
  and cut into thin rings
6 cups cooked beans, canned
  or from scratch
  (see Bean Tutorial, page 99)
1/2 cup beef stock, canned
  (or from scratch (see Stock Tutorial,
  page 47)
1 tbsp chile powder, to taste
salt, to taste
black pepper, to taste
1/2 cup fresh cilantro, chopped,
  plus sprigs for garnish
salsa, commercial or from scratch
  (see recipes, pages 37–41)
lime wedges
4 to 6 hard-boiled eggs (optional)

Remove chorizo from its skin and sauté contents gently in heavy skillet. Add a bit of olive oil or lard if necessary. Lightly sauté (only 3–4 minutes at most), remove to a dish, and set aside. Use leftover grease to lightly sauté onions, garlic, celery, and peppers until just beginning to brown. Add beans and stock. Return chorizo to skillet and cook over moderate heat until everything is hot. Season with chile powder, salt, and pepper and cook 3–4 minutes. If mixture seems too dry, add a bit more broth. Just before serving stir in cilantro. Pile onto serving platter with a generous pile of salsa in the center. Garnish with cilantro sprigs and lime wedges. Hard-boiled egg wedges make a nice garnish if dish is served for breakfast or brunch.

❋ SERVES 8 TO 10

Beer Drinkers Bean Pot

NOTE: For this dish you will need a covered ceramic bean pot and a good, preferably dark, Mexican beer.

5 to 6 cups cooked beans, canned
    or from scratch (see Bean Tutorial,
    page 99)

2 tbsps chile seasoning

1 tbsp paprika

1 tbsp Italian seasoning

1 tsp cumin seeds

1/2 cup molasses

dry chile flakes, to taste

2 white or yellow onions,
    sliced into thin rings

8 to 10 cloves garlic, sliced thin

2 red bell peppers, seeded
    and cut into thin rings

dark Mexican beer

beef stock, canned or from scratch
  (see Stock Tutorial, page 47)

salt, to taste

black pepper, to taste

1 cup mozzarella cheese, grated

1/2 cup fresh cilantro, chopped

Preheat oven to 325 degrees. In large bowl mix together beans, chile seasoning, paprika, Italian seasoning, cumin seeds, molasses, and chile flakes. Put a layer of bean mixture in a bean pot, cover with a layer each of onions, garlic, and peppers. Continue until ingredients are used, ending with beans. Mix beer and stock together and pour enough into the bean pot so beans are submerged but no liquid is standing above them. Cover with tight-fitting lid and bake until most liquid has been absorbed but beans are still moist, about 2 1/2–3 hours. The time will vary greatly, so keep checking. Season with salt and pepper and fold in cheese and cilantro. Return to oven, uncovered, and increase heat to 400 degrees. Bake a few minutes longer or until cheese is melted and just beginning to brown. This is a good dish for a buffet or potluck because it can sit in a warm oven until ready to serve.

❀ SERVES 8 TO 10

Rancheros Rice

This is an excellent side dish that also goes well with breakfast.

2 tbsps olive oil

2 onions, chopped

6 to 8 cloves garlic, minced

1 Anaheim chile, chopped

2 cups long grain white rice, uncooked

2 cups chile sauce

chicken, beef, or vegetarian stock,
  or from scratch (see Stock Tutorial,
  page 47)

salt, to taste

black pepper, to taste

1/4 cup fresh cilantro, chopped

Heat oil in large skillet with tight-fitting lid and gently sauté onion and garlic until pinkish and translucent. Do not brown. Add chile and continue to sauté 1–2 minutes. Add rice and stir until all grains are coated with oil. Add chile sauce and stir. Pour in enough stock to stand about 1 inch above rice. Cook over moderate heat until liquid has evaporated to the top of the rice. Turn off heat and cover with lid. Let sit 35–40 minutes. Remove lid and quickly add cilantro. Fluff rice with fork. Cover and let sit 5 minutes.

❀ SERVES 6 TO 8

Green Rice

2 to 3 tbsps olive oil

2 medium yellow onions, diced

6 to 8 cloves garlic, minced

1 cup salsa verde, commercial
  or from scratch (see recipe, page 41)

2 cups long grain white rice, uncooked

  chicken stock, canned or from scratch
  (see Stock Tutorial, page 47)

1/4 cup fresh cilantro, chopped

salt, to taste

black pepper, to taste

Heat oil in heavy skillet and lightly sauté onion and garlic. Add salsa and stir until hot. Add rice and stir to coat evenly. Smooth surface of rice with the back of a wooden spoon and gently pour in enough stock to stand about 1 inch above the rice. Bring to boil and cook until liquid is level with rice surface. Cover with tight-fitting lid and remove from heat. Let sit 40–45 minutes. Remove lid, fluff rice with fork, and gently stir in cilantro. Cover and let sit 5 minutes. Season with salt and pepper.

❀ SERVES 6 TO 8

Rice with Tomatoes and Cheese

2 to 3 tbsps olive oil

1 large yellow onion, chopped

6 to 8 cloves garlic, chopped

3 to 4 tomatoes, chopped

1 tbsp chile powder

1/2 tsp cumin seeds

1/2 tsp Mexican or regular oregano

1/2 tsp dry chile flakes, to taste

2 cups long grain white rice, uncooked

beef, chicken, or vegetarian stock,
   canned or from scratch
   (see Stock Tutorial, page 47)

1/2 cup fresh cilantro, chopped

1/2 cup sharp cheddar cheese, grated

1/2 cup mozzarella cheese, grated

1/2 cup queso fresco or feta cheese,
   crumbled

salt, to taste

 black pepper, to taste

Heat oil in heavy skillet and gently sauté onion and garlic until soft and light golden brown. Add tomatoes, chile powder, cumin seeds, oregano, and chile flakes; continue to sauté until hot. Add rice and stir to coat evenly. Smooth top of mixture and gently pour in enough stock to stand about 1 inch above rice. Bring to gentle boil and continue to boil until liquid is level with surface of rice. Remove from heat and cover immediately with tight-fitting lid. Let sit 40–45 minutes. Remove lid, fluff rice with fork, add cilantro and cheeses, and season with salt and pepper. Cover with lid and let sit 5 minutes. Remove lid, sprinkle with cheese, and put under broiler until cheese melts and begins to brown.

✿ SERVES 6 TO 8

Ranchero  Skillet Potatoes

4 to 6 potatoes

2 to 3 tbsps
   olive oil

2 large yellow onions, cut into thin rings

8 to 10 cloves garlic, chopped

1 small hot chile, seeded and cut into
   thin rings

1 Anaheim chile, seeded and cut into
   thin rings

1 red bell pepper, seeded and diced

1 green bell pepper, seeded and diced

1 tbsp chile powder

1 tbsp paprika

dry chile flakes, to taste

1 tsp Italian seasoning

1/2 cup fresh cilantro, chopped

salt, to taste

black pepper, to taste

Boil potatoes until they can be pierced with a cooking fork yet still offer some resistance; peel and cut into large dice. Heat oil in heavy skillet and sauté onions, garlic, chiles, and peppers until just beginning to brown. Add potatoes and continue to sauté until potatoes are nicely browned on all sides. You may need to add a bit more oil. About halfway though the cooking, add chile powder, paprika, chile flakes, and Italian seasoning. Continue sautéing until potatoes are done to your liking. Add cilantro just before cooking is finished, season with salt and pepper, and toss lightly.

❁ SERVES 6 TO 8

Potato & Egg Tortilla

4 potatoes

1 large white onion, diced small

6 to 8 cloves garlic, minced

1/4 cup fresh cilantro, chopped

1 tbsp chile powder, to taste

dry chile flakes, to taste

salt, to taste

black pepper, to taste

4 or 5 eggs, lightly beaten

olive oil

Peel and boil potatoes until outer 1/4 inch is done. When cool enough to handle, grate potatoes on large-hole side of hand grater. Add onion, garlic, cilantro, chile powder, chile flakes, salt, and pepper; mix gently. Fold eggs into mixture. Heat oil in heavy 9- or 10-inch nonstick skillet. Fry mixture undisturbed over moderate heat until moisture on top has dried and bottom is golden brown. Check color by gently lifting one side with spatula. Invert onto plate; gently slide back into skillet to brown other side. Slide onto serving platter, cut into wedges, and serve hot or cold. Serve with grilled sausages and fried eggs for a great breakfast or brunch dish.

❁ SERVES 6 TO 8

Grilled Corn on the Cob with Fiesta Butter

1 stick butter, softened
2 cloves garlic, very finely minced
1 tbsp fresh cilantro, minced
1 tsp chile powder
pinch dry chile flakes, to taste
salt, to taste
black pepper, to taste

Blend all ingredients together. When ready to grill corn, pull back husks but do not remove. Remove all silk. Rub each ear with mixture. Pull husks up and tie with several thin strips of husk. Place corn in bucket or pot of cold water and let sit about 30 minutes. (Soaking keeps husks from burning and helps steam corn when it's on the grill.) Place soaked ears on grill and roast 5–10 minutes, depending on size, turning occasionally. Be careful of sputtering water when placing on corn on hot grill. Remove one corn and test for doneness Goes well with grilled or barbecued meats.

❀ SERVES 6 TO 8

Corn Cakes

1 1/2 cups flour
1 1/2 cups Masa Harina
1 cup yellow cornmeal
2 tbsps baking powder
1 tsp salt
1/2 cup sugar
2 cups corn kernels, fresh or frozen
3 eggs, separated
1/4 cup olive oil, plus additional for frying
cold water

Combine flour, Masa Harina, cornmeal, baking powder, salt, and sugar in large bowl. Add corn and toss gently; set aside. Beat egg whites until stiff. Beat yolks with oil until creamy. Add yolk mixture to dry ingredients with just enough cold water to form thick pancake-like batter. Gently fold in egg whites. Heat enough oil to lightly coat bottom of heavy skillet or grilltop and drop batter by spoonfuls to cook like pancakes. Serve hot with sweet or savory toppings — syrup for breakfast or salsa and sour cream for side dish. Adding chopped onion, chopped fresh cilantro, and a dash of chile powder to the batter is a tasty savory variation.

❀ MAKES 2 TO 3 DOZEN DEPENDING ON SIZE

Fiesta Pumpkin Surprises

8 to 10 mini-pumpkins

2 tbsps olive oil

1 medium yellow onion, chopped small

4 to 6 cloves garlic, minced

2 tomatoes, chopped

1 tsp Italian seasoning

1 tsp chile powder

1/2 tsp cumin seeds, crushed

2 tbsps sugar, to taste

3 cups long grain white rice,
cooked al dente

1/4 cup pine nuts, shelled

1/4 cup currants

1/4 cup fresh parsley, chopped

salt, to taste

black pepper, to taste

2 eggs, lightly beaten

1/2 cup water, wine, or stock
(see Stock Tutorial, page 47)

cheese, grated (optional)

NOTE: Use all pumpkins in case some break during cooking.

Put pumpkins in large pot and boil until toothpick barely pierces them. Immediately plunge into cold water to stop cooking. When cool, carefully cut off tops and gently scoop out seeds. Set pumpkins aside to drain thoroughly. Heat olive oil in heavy skillet and gently sauté onion and garlic until just beginning to brown around edges. Add tomatoes, Italian seasoning, chile powder, cumin seeds, and sugar; continue to sauté 2–3 minutes. Add rice, pine nuts, currants, and parsley. Season with salt and pepper; stir in eggs. Stuff pumpkins generously with mixture. Place in baking dish with tight-fitting lid, add water, wine, or stock; cover and bake in 350-degree oven 30–45 minutes or until pumpkins are quite tender but not falling apart. If desired, top pumpkins with a bit of cheese just before they are done; bake uncovered until cheese melts.

❁ SERVES 6 TO 8

Corn Pudding

1 1/2 cups flour

1 cup Masa Harina

1 cup yellow cornmeal

2 tbsps baking powder

1 tsp Italian seasoning

1 tsp chile powder, to taste

salt, to taste

black pepper, to taste

1 1/2 cups cheddar cheese, grated

1/4 cup fresh cilantro, chopped

4 eggs, separated

1/4 cup olive oil

milk

Preheat oven to 350 degrees. Mix all dry ingredients together. Add cheese and cilantro. Beat egg whites until stiff. Beat yolks with oil until creamy. Add yolk mixture to dry ingredients and gently beat in enough milk to form medium-thick batter. Gently fold in egg whites and pour into oiled baking dish large enough for 30 percent expansion. Bake 30 minutes or until a toothpick inserted in the center comes out clean. Serve hot.

✿ SERVES 6 TO 8

Sizzling Zucchini Cornbread

4 tbsps olive oil, divided, plus additional for frying

1 cup flour

1 cup Masa Harina

1 cup yellow cornmeal

1/4 cup sugar

1 tbsp chile powder

1 tsp Italian seasoning

dry chile flakes, to taste

salt, to taste

black pepper, to taste

3 eggs, lightly beaten

1 1/2 cups zucchini, grated

cold water

Preheat oven to 500 degrees. Pour 3 tablespoons olive oil into 8- or 9-inch cast-iron skillet and place in oven. Working quickly, combine all dry ingredients. Add eggs, remaining tablespoon oil, zucchini, and enough cold water to form very stiff batter. Quickly remove skillet from oven and carefully pour in batter. (WARNING: Oil in skillet is very hot. Be careful not to spill it, and be careful of splattering.) Replace skillet in oven immediately so temperature does not drop too much. Bake 5 minutes, reduce heat to 350 degrees, and bake 35–45 minutes or until toothpick inserted in the center comes out clean. Remove from oven and let sit 5 minutes before cutting into wedges. Serve hot.

✿ MAKES ONE 8- TO 9-INCH SKILLET

Blue Cornbread

4 tbsps olive oil, divided,
   plus additional for frying

1 1/2 cups flour

1 1/2 cups blue cornmeal

1/4 cup sugar

1 tbsp baking powder

salt, to taste

3 eggs, lightly beaten

cold water

Preheat oven to 500 degrees. Pour 3 tablespoons oil into 8- or 9-inch cast-iron skillet and place in oven. Working quickly, combine all dry ingredients. Add eggs, oil, and enough cold water to make thick batter. Quickly remove skillet from oven and carefully pour in batter. (WARNING: Oil in skillet is very hot. Be careful not to spill it, and be careful of splattering.) Replace skillet in oven immediately so temperature does not drop too much. Bake 5 minutes, reduce heat to 350 degrees, and bake 35–45 minutes or until toothpick inserted in the center comes out clean. Remove from oven and let sit 5 minutes before cutting into wedges. Serve hot.

❉ MAKES ONE 8- TO 9-INCH FULL SKILLET

Postres

Desserts

Fiesta Dessert Empanadas

1/2 cup candied pineapple, finely chopped

1/2 cup dry currants

1/2 cup candied papaya, finely chopped

1/4 cup candied ginger, finely chopped

1/4 cup shelled pine nuts

2 tbsps dark molasses

1 tbsp rum extract

empanada pastry, unbaked
  (see recipe, page 30)

1 egg beaten with 1 tbsp water

raw sugar

Preheat oven to 450 degrees. Mix pineapple, currants, papaya, ginger, pine nuts, molasses, and rum together well and set aside. Roll pastry out to about 1/8-inch thick. Cut into 4-inch rounds. Place a heaping tablespoon of the filling on each round, being careful not to get any on the outer edge. Paint outer edge with the egg-water wash. Fold pastry in half to form a crescent and crimp edges with fork tines to seal. Place empanadas about 1 inch apart on a baking sheet lined with baker's parchment. Paint each surface with the egg-water wash and sprinkle with raw (not brown) sugar. Use a small sharp knife to make one or two small slits in the top of each empanada. Bake 5 minutes, then reduce heat to 350 degrees. Continue to bake until empanadas are golden brown, about 20–25 minutes. Cool completely before wrapping and storing or eating.

❋ MAKES 16 TO 20

Totally Decadent Chocolate Mousse

2 large eggs

1 cup sugar

1/2 cup dark rum

1/2 tsp cinnamon

1 tbsp Mexican vanilla

1 package semisweet chocolate chips

2 cups half & half

1/2 pint plus additional whipping cream

shaved bittersweet chocolate

Separate eggs and set whites aside. Put yolks into the top of a double boiler with sugar, rum, cinnamon, vanilla, chocolate chips, and half & half. Whisk while cooking gently. Cook until mixture has thickened and chocolate has melted. Set aside to cool. Beat egg whites until stiff. In a separate bowl, whip 1/2 pint whipping cream until stiff but not dry; set aside. Add about 1/4 of the beaten egg whites to the cooled chocolate mixture and fold in to lighten the mixture (this is called tempering). Gently fold this mixture back into remaining egg whites. Then gently and slowly fold this mixture into whipped cream. Pile into individual serving dishes and chill throroughly until cold. When ready to serve, whip additional whipping cream and put a dollop on each serving. Top cream with a few shavings of bittersweet chocolate.

❋ SERVES 6 TO 8

Basic Flan

Basic flan is found from one end of Mexico to the other. There are numerous recipes with delightful regional variations, but they all start from a basic milk and egg baked custard.

1 quart half & half (see Note)
1 cup sugar
1 tsp vanilla
1/2 tsp ground nutmeg
6 eggs, beaten well

Preheat oven to 325 degrees. Mix all ingredients together well. Pour into a mold or baking dish large enough (1 1/2 to 2 quart) to hold all ingredients comfortably. Bake in a water bath about 1 1/2 hours or until a knife inserted into the center comes out clean. Allow to cool and then refrigerate until chilled before unmolding. To unmold, slide a table knife around the inside rim of the baking dish. Set the bottom of the baking dish in hot water for a quick second or two. Place a large serving plate over the top of the baking dish and invert. The flan should slide out nicely.

NOTE: For a lighter version use milk instead of half & half. For a richer version use cream, or add cream to half & half to make 1 quart.

For a delicious variation add 1 cup canned pumpkin, 1 teaspoon cinnamon, and 1/2 teaspoon powdered ginger to ingredients. Follow the same directions, and sprinkle the top with shelled pumpkin seeds before baking.

❀ SERVES 6 TO 8

Sweet Tooth Candied Pumpkin

3 cups of fresh pumpkin, peeled and
  cut into 1/2 x 1 x 2-inch pieces

2 cups of sugar

1 cup of light corn syrup

1/2 cup water

2 to 3 cinnamon sticks

2 to 3 slices fresh ginger root

salt

Bring a pot of lightly salted water to
the boil and carefully slide in the cut
pumpkin. Boil for about 2 minutes
only. Drain immediately and cool in
cold running water. Drain well and set
aside. Put all remaining ingredients
into a pot and bring to the boil.
Reduce to a simmer and cook for
about 15 minutes. Add the drained
pumpkin, bring back to a boil, then
reduce to a simmer and cook for
about 5 minutes only. Remove from
the heat, cover and allow to sit, unre-
frigerated, overnight. The next day,

return to the boil, reduce to a simmer
and cook for only about 2 minutes,
then remove from the heat, cover and
allow to sit overnight again. Continue
doing this for 2 or 3 more days or
until the pumpkin is translucent and
has been completely penetrated by
the syrup. Taste a piece to test. When
finished, drain and set the pieces of
pumpkin on a wire rack over a
piece of wax paper to drain. Leave
to air dry over night or until the
surface is only tacky. Roll in sugar
and store in an air tight jar. Serve
as candy.

❀ MAKES ABOUT 3 CUPS

Pound Cake

Pound cake is the starting point for many wonderful desserts. A slice of pound cake with a spoonful of fresh fruit compote is excellent. Pound cake with ice cream and a dribbling of liquor is elegant and easy. Trifles and tipsy cakes are a long-standing tradition in Mexican cuisine, and pound cake is the base for them.

1 pound (2 cups or 4 sticks) butter
  or margarine
1 pound (2 cups) sugar
1 pound (10 to 12) eggs
1 tsp nutmeg
1 tsp vanilla or almond extract
1 pound (4 cups) flour

Preheat oven to 325 degrees. Melt butter and let cool. Beat sugar and eggs together with a wire whisk or rotary beater. Add nutmeg, vanilla or almond extract, and cooled butter. Beat until smooth, creamy, and completely mixed. Gradually add flour a few tablespoons at a time, thoroughly incorporating after each addition. Pour into two oiled and floured loaf pans and bake about 1 hour or until a toothpick inserted into the center comes out clean. Set the pans on a wire rack and cool before removing. Goes well with a variety of elements, from fruit and liquor to chocolate sauce and ice cream. Toasting before topping is another tasty technique.

❁ MAKES 2 LOAF CAKES

NOTE:
For festive occasions in Mexico, brightly colored bits of dried fruit (cherries, papaya, mango, etc.) are added before baking.

Rice Pudding

3 cups cooked rice, cold
2 cups milk or half & half
4 eggs, beaten
1/2 cup dried currants
1/4 cup candied ginger, slivered
1 tsp vanilla
1 tsp cinnamon
1 tsp nutmeg
zest of 1 lemon
dried fruits (see Note)

Preheat oven to 350 degrees. Mix all ingredients together and pour into a baking dish large enough to hold mixture comfortably (1 1/2 to 2 quart baking dish). Set dish into a water bath and bake about 1 1/2 hours or until top is a light golden brown and a table knife inserted in the center comes out clean. Serve hot or cold. This is very good with thick cream poured over each serving.

❁ SERVES 6 TO 8

Almond Cookies

1 cup sugar
1 cup (1/2 pound or 2 sticks) butter
1 egg, lightly beaten
4 cups flour
1 cup blanched almonds, finely chopped

Preheat oven to 325 degrees. Blend sugar and butter together thoroughly. Add egg and incorporate well. Add flour and nuts and mix well; you may have to use your hands for this part. Press into pie pans to 1/2-inch thickness. Prick the surface all over with a fork. Bake about 1 hour or until the cookies are a pale buff color, not brown. Remove from oven and use the back of a large wooden spoon to press together any cracks on cookie surface. While still warm cut into slim, pie-shaped wedges and leave in pan to cool. When cool, lift out of pans and store in airtight containers (like large glass jars) until ready to use. The cookies taste much better if they are made at least a week before you need them.

✺ MAKES ABOUT 2 DOZEN

Day of the Dead Sugar Skulls

1 large egg, separated

2 tbsps water

4 cups sugar

Lightly beat egg white with water. Add sugar and mix thoroughly. Use this sugar compound to pack into the molds. I use the larger two-piece full-head molds purchased through online resources.

NOTE: You can hasten the drying process by putting the skulls in the oven. If you have a gas oven, leave the door open a bit; even the heat from the pilot light can turn the skulls a bit brown. If you have an electric oven, use the very lowest heat with the door slightly open; keep checking the molds. When possible it's best to air dry. When completely dry, use small sharp knife to smooth the edges and glue halves together with Royal Icing (see recipe to right).

Two packing methods:

1. This is the easier method. First, spray molds with nonstick spray. Pack them full with sugar mixture and smooth surface as much as possible. Make sure to pack them well to maintain the molds' details. Turn molds onto baking sheets lined with bakers' parchment. Put baking sheets in a warm, not hot place at least 48 hours or until molds are thoroughly dry. Put the two pieces together with Royal Icing.

2. This method is a bit more tedious, but the skulls dry more quickly and not as much sugar is wasted. First, spray molds with non-stick spray. Pack each mold half with the sugar compound, then use a teaspoon and very carefully scoop out the sugar in the center of the mold, leaving at least a 1/2-inch thick shell. Carefully flip the mold over onto the baking sheet lined with baker's parchment. Sometimes when you flip the skull it will break and you must scoop up the sugar compound and begin again.

Royal Icing

1 large egg, separated

1 tbsp water

powdered sugar, sifted

Lightly beat egg white with water. Mix in powdered sugar until desired texture is achieved. To glue skull halves together, icing must be consistency of extremely thick cream. If using a frosting bag, icing must be thick enough to maintain its shape but not so thick that it can't be squeezed out.

NOTE: Sealed sandwich bags work well as frosting bags when a small portion of a corner is cut off to make a tip. Use colored icing when decorating and create using food coloring. Cake decorating jells work even better.

Sopapillas

3 tbsps butter
2 cups flour
1 cup warm (not hot) water
vegetable oil
powdered sugar
cinnamon

Cut butter into small pieces and add to flour. Using pastry blender, work butter into flour until mixture is powdery. With fork begin working in enough water to form soft dough. Turn dough onto floured work surface and knead well, at least 5 minutes. Form into ball, cover with plastic, and let rest about 30 minutes. Form dough into rope about 1 inch in diameter. Cut off chunks and form into 1-inch balls. Put about 1/2 inch vegetable oil in heavy skillet and heat to deep frying temperature [360 to 375 degrees]. Sprinkle a bit more flour on work surface and flatten one ball into disk shape. Working carefully, use rolling pin and roll into circle about 4 inches in diameter. Do the same with 2 or 3 balls. Cut each circle into 4–6 triangles. Drop a few triangles into hot oil. They should puff up in about 2 seconds. Fry on one side until light golden brown. Turn over and fry other side. Be aware that these will fry very quickly. Drain on platter covered with paper towels. Continue until all balls are rolled and fried. While still warm sprinkle with powdered sugar.

NOTE: Make a quick and easy version by cutting flour tortillas into triangles and frying them the same way, then dusting with powdered sugar.

❁ MAKES 2 TO 3 DOZEN

Fried Fruit

about 3 cups fresh fruit of choice, such as bananas, papayas, orange segments, pineapple, apples
lemon or lime juice
1/2 cup sugar
1/2 stick butter
1/2 cup inexpensive cream Sherry
1 tbsp molasses
1 tsp powdered ginger
sesame seeds

Peel fruit if necessary and cut into bite-size chunks. Sprinkle with a bit of lemon or lime juice to prevent browning; cover with plastic until ready to use. Place sugar, butter, Sherry, molasses, and ginger into heavy skillet; simmer over moderate heat until mixture becomes thin syrup. Place a few pieces of fruit at a time into syrup and simmer gently on both sides until evenly coated. Remove to warm serving dish and sprinkle lightly with sesame seeds. Continue until all fruit has been cooked. Fruit is delicious as is or with thick cream poured over the top.

❁ SERVES 4 TO 6

Bebidas

Beverages

Margarita

A perfect margarita cannot be achieved with a bottle of premade mix. The ingredients should be pure and fresh.

1 lime, sliced thin, divided
salt
juice of 1 lime
1 1/2 oz. tequila (I prefer gold)
1 oz. Triple Sec
4 to 6 ice cubes

Rub the rim of a large cocktail glass with a slice of lime. Place salt on a plate and press the rim of the glass into the salt to coat the rim evenly. Chill the glass. Put lime juice, tequila, Triple Sec, and ice cubes into a blender and process until the mix has turned slushy. Pour into the chilled glass, garnish with a thin slice of lime, and serve immediately.

✿ SERVES 1

Tequila Sunrise

There are a lot of Tequila Sunrise concoctions that claim to be the best, but my favorite is the simplest.

1 lime, sliced
salt
ice, crushed
4 oz. tequila
2 cups fresh orange juice
1 oz. grenadine
ice cubes
1 orange, sliced
fresh mint sprigs

Rub the rims of two tall glasses with a slice of lime. Place salt on a plate and press the rim of each glass into the salt to coat the rim evenly. Fill the glasses with crushed ice. Pour tequila, orange juice, and grenadine into a pitcher with ice cubes, stir, and strain into the prepared glasses. Garnish with orange slice and mint.

✿ SERVES 2

Bloody Maria

1 lime, sliced and divided
1 shot (1 oz.) tequila
dash Worcestershire sauce
dash hot sauce
dash celery salt
ice cubes
Clamato juice
  (1/2 tomato juice,
  1/2 clam nectar)
1 celery stalk

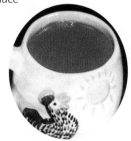

Rub the rim of a tall glass with a slice of lime. Place salt on a plate and press the rim of the glass into the salt to coat the rim evenly. Mix tequila, Worcestershire sauce, hot sauce, and celery salt in the glass and add several ice cubes. Fill the glass with Clamato juice and stir well. Garnish with celery and lime slice.

✿ SERVES 1

Classic Sangria

There appear to be as many recipes for Sangria as there are people who have experimented with it. Some varieties are delectable, and some, to my way of thinking, are really wretched. This one will keep the party going!

4 cups orange juice
1 cup lime juice
1/4 cup grenadine
1 cup sherry
1/2 cup tequila
pinch salt
pinch cayenne pepper
ice cubes
1 lemon, sliced (optional)
1 lime, sliced (optional)
fresh mint sprigs (optional)

Mix together orange juice, lime juice, grenadine, sherry, tequila, salt, and pepper. Pour into a large pitcher filled with ice cubes. Garnish the pitcher with lemon and lime slices and fresh mint sprigs, if desired. This is truly a great cooler.

✸ SERVES 4

Carmen Miranda Fruit Punch

2 quarts reconstituted tropical fruit punch made with lemon-lime soda instead of water
3 cups red table wine
1 cup tequila
6 limes, juiced
1 orange, sliced
2 limes, sliced
2 or 3 slices pineapple
fresh mint sprigs
ice cubes

Put punch, wine, tequila, and lime juice in a pitcher. Mix well and refrigerate until chilled. Add orange and lime slices and mint sprigs. To serve, put ice into tall glasses and pour punch over ice.

✸ SERVES 8 TO 10

Beyond Carrot Juice

NOTE: This recipe requires an electric juicer.

10 carrots, cut into pieces
4 apples, cut into eighths with seeds removed
2 beets, cut into pieces
1/2-inch-slice fresh ginger root
ice cubes
1 lime

Run carrots, apples, beets, and ginger through the juicer. Put juice into a jar and refrigerate until thoroughly chilled. Serve over ice cubes in tall glasses with a squeeze of lime.

SERVES 3 TO 4

Tropical Smoothie

1 cup fresh pineapple, cubed

1 small papaya, peeled and diced

1 cup strawberries, chopped

1 cup ice cubes

2 cups half & half or milk

fresh berries (strawberries are good,
   or your choice)

fresh mint sprigs

Blend pineapple, papaya, chopped
strawberries, ice, and half & half until
the ice is thoroughly blended. Pour
into chilled tall glasses. Garnish with
berries and mint sprigs.

❊ SERVES 3 TO 4

Fabulous Fiesta Coffee Freeze

1 cup cold, dark-roast brewed coffee

1 tbsp instant cocoa

1/4 tsp cinnamon

sugar, to taste (1 to 2 tbsps)

1/2 cup cream

1 cup ice cubes

Blend all ingredients until the ice is blended.
Pour into a chilled tall glass and serve immediately.

❁ SERVES 1

NOTE:
Although this is usually a nonalcoholic drink, it certainly is not damaged by adding a shot of brandy or Kalua.

Breakfast Fiesta Coffee

1 tbsp dark semisweet chocolate, grated

1/2 tsp Mexican or regular vanilla

pinch cinnamon

brown sugar, to taste

1 large mug 2/3 full of strong, hot, dark-roast brewed coffee

half & half

Add chocolate, vanilla, cinnamon, and brown sugar to coffee in mug. Add half & half to within 1 inch of the top and whisk to a froth. Serve immediately.

NOTE:
You may also whip in a blender.

❁ SERVES 1

Clean as a whistle

Rompope (Mexican Eggnog)

Many people are apprehensive about consuming raw eggs in any form. In fact, the risk of getting sick from eating raw eggs is far less than the risk of being killed or injured in your car on the way to the store to get the eggs.

12 very fresh eggs, divided

2 cups sugar

2 tbsps vanilla extract

2 tsps nutmeg, plus additional for sprinkling

2 quarts half & half or milk

Note: For eggnog with an extra kick, add 1 cup of rum.

Separate 4 eggs and set the whites aside. Combine yolks with remaining eggs in a large bowl. Beat with a wire whisk until golden, thick, and creamy. Add sugar, vanilla, and nutmeg and continue beating until creamy. Begin whisking in half & half or milk until all is well incorporated. In a separate bowl beat egg whites until they hold soft peaks. Gently fold 2 cups of egg and half & half mixture into the beaten egg whites until well blended. Gradually add this mixture to the remaining egg and half & half mixture, folding in gently. Serve chilled in a bowl with nutmeg sprinkled on top.

❄ SERVES 8 TO 10

Index